# THE
# CHANGING ROOM

DAVID STOREY

PENGUIN BOOKS

Penguin Books Ltd, Harmondsworth, Middlesex, England
Penguin Books Australia Ltd, Ringwood, Victoria Australia

—

First published Jonathan Cape 1972
Published in Penguin Books 1973

—

Copyright © David Storey, 1972

—

Made and printed in Great Britain by
Cox & Wyman Ltd,
London, Reading and Fakenham
Set in Monotype Bembo

—

TO JAKE

This play was first presented at the Royal Court Theatre, London, on November 9th, 1971, under the direction of Lindsay Anderson. The cast was as follows:

| | |
|---|---|
| Harry | JOHN BARRETT |
| Patsy | JIM NORTON |
| Fielding | DAVID DAKER |
| Mic Morley | EDWARD PEEL |
| Kendal | WARREN CLARKE |
| Luke | DON MCKILLOP |
| Fenchurch | PETER CHILDS |
| Colin Jagger | MARK MCMANUS |
| Trevor | MICHAEL ELPHICK |
| Walsh | EDWARD JUDD |
| Sandford | BRIAN GLOVER |
| Barry Copley | GEOFFREY HINSLIFF |
| Jack Stringer | DAVID HILL |
| Bryan Atkinson | PETER SCHOFIELD |
| Billy Spencer | ALUN ARMSTRONG |
| John Clegg | MATTHEW GUINNESS |
| Frank Moore | JOHN PRICE |
| Danny Crosby | BARRY KEEGAN |
| Cliff Owens | FRANK MILLS |
| Tallon | BRIAN LAWSON |
| Thornton | PAUL DAWKINS |
| Mackendrick | JOHN RAE |

# CHARACTERS

| | |
|---|---|
| HARRY | Cleaner: 50–60 |
| PATSY | Wing threequarter: 23–5 |
| FIELDING | Forward: 35–6 |
| Mic MORLEY | Forward: 28 |
| KENDAL | Forward: 29 |
| LUKE | Masseur: 40–50 |
| FENCHURCH | Wing threequarter: 23–5 |
| Colin JAGGER | Centre threequarter: 26 |
| TREVOR | Full-back: 26 |
| WALSH | Forward: 35–40 |
| SANDFORD | Assistant trainer: 40 |
| Barry COPLEY | Scrum-half: 27–8 |
| Jack STRINGER | Centre threequarter: 30 |
| Bryan ATKINSON | Forward: 32 |
| Billy SPENCER | Reserve: 20 |
| John CLEGG | Hooker: 30 |
| Frank MOORE | Reserve: 21 |
| Danny CROSBY | Trainer: 45–50 |
| Cliff OWENS | Stand-off half: 30–32 |
| TALLON | Referee |
| THORNTON | Chairman: 50 |
| MACKENDRICK | Club Secretary: 60 |

# ACT ONE

*A changing room; afternoon. The light comes from glazed panels
high in the wall and from an electric light.*

*Across the back of the stage is the main changing bench, set up
against the wall and running its entire length. A set of hooks, one
for each player, is fastened at head height to the wall, with the
name of a player above each hook. Underneath the bench, below
each hook, is a locker, also labelled. A jersey and a pair of shorts
have been set out beneath one of the hooks. A rubbing-down table
with an adjustable head-rest stands in front of the bench. Stage
right, a glazed door opens to an entrance porch. Downstage left is
a fireplace, with a bucket of coal, overhung by a mirror advertising
ale. Upstage left is the open entry to the bath and showers: buckets,
stool, hose and tap, etc. Downstage right is a wooden door,
closed, leading to the offices. A second table stands against the
wall. There's a pair of metal scales with individual metal weights
on a metal arm. By the rubbing-down table stands a large wickerwork basket. A wooden chair with a rounded back is set against the
wall, stage left.*

*Tannoy music is being played, light, militaristic.*

HARRY *enters from the bath. He's a broken-down man, small,
stooped, in shirt-sleeves, rolled, and a sleeveless pullover. He's
smoking and carries a sweeping-brush, on the lookout for anything
he might have missed. He sweeps, looks round the floor, sweeps;
finally lifts corner of the boxed-in rubbing-down table and sweeps
the debris underneath. Takes out his cigarette, looks round, finds
nowhere to drop it, then crosses to the fire; drops it in, sets the
brush against the wall, puts coal from the bucket on the fire, warms
his hands, shivers.*

PATSY *enters from the porch. He's a smart, lightly built man, very well groomed, hair greased, collar of an expensive overcoat turned up. Brisk, businesslike, narcissistic, no evident sense of humour.*

PATSY. Harry ...

HARRY. Patsy ...

PATSY. Cold.

HARRY. Bloody freezing, lad. (*Rubs his hands; reaches to the fire again.*)

  (PATSY, *evidently familiar with his routine, goes to his locker. Gets out his boots, unfolds his jersey and shorts already lying on the bench.*)

PATSY. No towel.

HARRY. No. No. Just fetching those ... (*Takes his brush and exits through bath entrance.*)

  (PATSY, *having checked his jersey, examined its number (2), collar, etc. — no marks — does the same with his boots: laces, studs, lining. He then crosses to the fire, takes out a comb from an inside pocket and smooths his hair down in the mirror. He's doing this as* HARRY *re-enters carrying several neatly folded towels. He puts one on the bench by* PATSY's *peg, then goes to the wickerwork basket, lifts the lid and gets out several more towels. Having checked them, counting soundlessly to himself, he puts them all in the basket, save three which he begins to arrange on the massage table.*

  PATSY, *having combed his hair and admired himself in the mirror, clears his nose and spits in the fire.*)

HARRY (*laying out towels*). Thought it'd be snowed off.

PATSY. Snow?

HARRY. Bloody forecast.

PATSY. Not cancel ought in this dump, I can tell you ... Shoulder ... I've no skin on from here to here. There's not a blade o' grass on that bloody pitch ... sithee ... look at that ...

(*Pulls up his sleeve.* HARRY *looks across with no evident interest.*)

HARRY. Aye.

PATSY. Watered t'bloody pitch we 'ad last week. Froze over ten minutes after. Took a run at t'bloody ball ... took off ... must have travelled twenty bloody yards without having lift a finger.

HARRY. Aye.

PATSY. Ice.

(HARRY *is laying out the rest of the jerseys now, and shorts.*)

PATSY. Be better off with a pair of skates. (*Glances behind him, into the mirror; smooths hair.*) If there's a young woman comes asking for me afterwards, will you tell her to wait up in the office? Be frozen to death out theer.

HARRY. Aye ...

PATSY. By Christ ... (*Rubs his hands, standing with his back to the fire.*)

HARRY. Comes from Russia.

PATSY. What?

HARRY. Cold ... Comes fro' Russia ...

PATSY. Oh ... (*Nods.*)

HARRY. Read a book ... they had a special machine ... blew these winds o'er, you see ... specially freezing ... mixed it with a chemical ... frozen ought ... Froze the entire country ... Then Ireland ... Then crossed over to America and froze it out ... Then, when everything wa' frozen, they came o'er in special boots and took over ... Here ... America ... Nobody twigged it. Nobody cottoned on, you see.

PATSY. Oh ... (*Glances at himself in mirror again.*) You think that's what's happening now, then?

HARRY. Cold enough ... Get no warning ... Afore you know what's happening ... Ruskies here.

PATSY. Couldn't be worse than this lot.

HARRY. What?

PATSY. Stopped ten quid i' bloody tax last week ... I tell you ... I'm paying t'government to keep me i' bloody work ... madhouse ... If I had my time o'er again I'd emigrate ... America ... Australia ...

HARRY. Wherever you go they'll find you out.

PATSY. What?

HARRY. Ruskies ... Keep your name down in a bloody book ... (*Looks across.*) Won't make any difference if you've voted socialist. Have you down theer ... up against a wall ...

PATSY. Thy wants to read one or two bloody facts, old lad.

HARRY. Facts? What facts? ... I read in one paper that in twenty-five years not one country on earth'll not be communist ...

> (PATSY *crosses back to his peg and starts taking off his overcoat.*)

Don't worry. There'll be no lakin' bloody football then.

PATSY. They lake football i' Russia as much as they lake it here.

HARRY. Aye ...

> (HARRY *waits, threatening;* PATSY *doesn't answer, pre-occupied with his overcoat.*)

You: football ... You: coalmine ... You: factory ... You: air-force ... You ... *Siberia.*

PATSY. Haven't you got a bloody coat-hanger? Damn well ask for one each week.

HARRY. Aye. Don't worry ... (*Starts to go.*) Not bloody listen until they find it's bloody well too late. (*Goes off to the bath entrance, disgruntled.*)

> (FIELDING *enters: large, well-built man, slow, easy-going, thirty-five to thirty-six. He's dressed in an overcoat and muffler; he has a strip of plaster above his left eye.*)

FIELDING. Patsy.

PATSY. Fieldy ...

FIELDING. Freeze your knuckles off today. (*Blows in hands, goes over to fire; stoops, warms hands.*) By Christ ...

>(PATSY *is holding up his coat in one hand, dusting it down lightly, paying no attention to* FIELDING'*s entrance.*
>HARRY *comes back in with wooden coat-hanger.*)

HARRY. Have no bloody servants theer, you know.

PATSY (*examining coat*). What's that?

HARRY. No servants. Do your own bloody carrying theer.

>(*Gives* PATSY *the hanger and goes back to laying out the playing-kit.*)

FIELDING. What's that, Harry? (*Winks to* PATSY.)

PATSY. Bloody Russians. Going to be invaded.

HARRY. Don't you worry. It can happen any time, you know.

PATSY. Going to freeze us, with a special liquid ... Then come over ... (*To* HARRY) What wa're it? ... i' special boots.

HARRY. It all goes back, you know.

PATSY. Back?

HARRY. To bloody Moscow ... Ought you say here's reported back ... Keep all thy names in a special book.

FIELDING. Keep thy name in a special bloody book ... Riley ... First name: Harry ... Special qualifications: can talk out of the back of his bloody head.

HARRY. Don't you worry.

FIELDING. Nay, I'm not worried. They can come here any day of the bloody week for me. Sup of ale ...

PATSY. Ten fags ...

FIELDING. That's all I need. (*Sneezes hugely. Shakes his head, gets out his handkerchief, blows his nose, lengthily and noisily.*) Come on, then, Harry ... Switch it off.

>(*After gazing at* FIELDING, *threatening,* HARRY *turns off the Tannoy.*)

I thought o' ringing up this morning ... Looked out o' the bloody winder. Frost ... (*Crosses over to* PATSY.) Got this house, now, just outside the town ... wife's idea, not mine ... bloody fields ... hardly a bloody sign of human life ... cows ... half a dozen sheep ... goats ...

(*Starts peeling the plaster from above his eye.* PATSY *pays no attention, arranging his coat on the hanger and picking off one or two bits.*)

Middle of bloody nowhere ... if I can't see a wall outside on t'window I don't feel as though I'm living in a house ... How's it look?

PATSY (*glances up, briefly*). All right.

FIELDING. Bloody fist. Loose forra'd ... Copped him one afore the end. Had a leg like a bloody melon ... (*Feeling the cut.*) Get Lukey to put on a bit of grease ... Should be all right. How's your shoulder?

PATSY. All right. (*Eases it.*) Came in early. Get it strapped. (*Indicates, however, that there's no one here.*)

FIELDING. Where we lived afore, you know, everything you could bloody want: pit, boozer, bloody dogs. As for now ... trees, hedges, miles o' bloody grass ... (*Inspecting his kit which* HARRY *has now hung up.*) Weer's the jock-straps, Harry? ... I thought of ringing up and backing out. Flu ... some such like. (*Sneezes.*) By God ... He'll have me lakin' here, will Harry, wi' me bloody cobblers hanging out.

(MORLEY *has now entered from the porch: thick-set, squat figure, dark-haired. Wears a jacket, unbuttoned, with a sweater underneath; hard, rough, uncomplicated figure.*)

Nah, Morley, lad, then: how's thy keeping?

MORLEY. Shan't be a second ... Just o'd on. (*Goes straight over to the bath entrance, unbuttoning his flies.*)

(*He's followed in by* KENDAL: *tall, rather well-built, late twenties, wearing an old overcoat with a scarf, and carrying*

14

*a paper parcel. A worn, somewhat faded man.*
HARRY *has gone to the basket and is now getting out a pile of jock-straps which he lays on the table.*)

KENDAL (*to* HARRY). Here ... see about my boots? Bloody stud missing last Thursday ... (*To* FIELDING) Suppose to check them every bloody week. Come up to training and nearly bust me bloody ankle. God Christ, they don't give a sod about bloody ought up here ... Patsy ...

PATSY. Kenny ... (*Having hung up his coat, starts taking off his jacket.*)

KENDAL (*to* FIELDING). Bought one of these electric tool-sets ...

FIELDING (*to* PATSY). Tool-sets ...
(PATSY *nods.*)

FIELDING. Got all the tools that I need, Kenny.

KENDAL. Bloody saw ... drill, bloody polisher. Just look.

FIELDING. What do you do with that? (*Picks out a tool.*)

KENDAL. Dunno.

PATSY. Take stones out of hosses' hoofs, more like.
(*They laugh.*
MORLEY *comes back in.*)

FIELDING. Dirty bugger. Pisses i' the bloody bath.

MORLEY. Been in that bog, then, have you? (*To* HARRY) You want to clean it out.

HARRY. That lavatory was new this season ... (*Indicating* FIELDING) He'll tell you. One we had afore I wouldn't have used.
(MORLEY *goes straight to the business of getting changed: coat off, sweater, then shoes and socks; then starts examining his ankle.*)

FIELDING. Harry doesn't use a lavatory, do you?

MORLEY. Piles it up behind the bloody posts.

FIELDING. Dirty bugger.

HARRY. Don't worry. It all goes down.

MORLEY. Goes down?
    (*They laugh.*)
    Goes down where, then, lad?

PATSY. He's reporting it back, tha knows, to Moscow.

MORLEY. Moscow? Moscow?

HARRY. Somebody does, don't you bloody worry. Every-thing they hear.

FIELDING. Nay, Harry, lad. Thy should have warned us. (*Puts his arm round* HARRY'S *shoulder.*)

HARRY. Don't worry. You carry on. (*Breaks away from* FIELDING'S *embrace.*) You'll be laughing t'other side of your bloody face. (*Exits.*)

FIELDING (*holding jersey up*). Given me number four, an' all. I'll be all right jumping up and down i' middle o' yon bloody backs.

KENDAL. By God (*rubbing his hands at the fire*). I wouldn't mind being on the bloody bench today.
    (*Pause.* LUKE *comes in, wearing a track-suit and baseball shoes and carrying a large hold-all, plus a large tin of Vaseline; sets them down by the massage table. A small, middle-aged man, perky, brisk, grey-haired.*)

FIELDING. Nah, Lukey, lad. Got a drop o' rum in theer, then, have you?

LUKE. Aye. Could do with it today.

MORLEY. Lukey ...

KENDAL. Lukey ...

LUKE. Who's first on, then? (*Indicating the table.*) By Christ ... (*Rubs his hands.*)

PATSY. My bloody shoulder ...

LUKE. Aye. Right, then. Let's have a look. (*Rummaging in his bag; gets out crepe bandage.*)
    (PATSY *is stripped to his shirt by now; takes it off, hangs it and comes over in his vest and trousers. Sits on the edge of table for* LUKE *to strap him up.*)

MORLEY. Bloody ankle, Lukey ...

LUKE. Aye. All right.

FIELDING (*examining* PATSY'*s shoulder*). By God, there's nowt theer, lad. Which shoulder wa're it?

MORLEY. Sprained it.

FIELDING. Sprained it.

MORLEY. Twisted it i' bed.

> (*They laugh.* PATSY *pays no attention. Holds his elbow as if one shoulder gives him great pain.*
> HARRY *comes back in with remaining jerseys.*)

LUKE. Right, then, lad. Let's have it off.

> (*Having got out all his equipment,* LUKE *helps* PATSY *off with his vest.*)

KENDAL (*to* MORLEY). Look at that, then, eh? (*Shows him his tool-kit.*) Sand-paper ... polisher ... circular saw ...

FIELDING (*stripping*). What're you going to mek with that, then, Kenny?

KENDAL. Dunno ... shelves.

MORLEY. What for?

KENDAL. Books.

FIELDING (*laughs*). Thy's never read a bleeding book.

KENDAL. The wife reads ... Got three or four at home.

> (MORLEY *laughs.*)

Cupboards ... Any amount o' things ... Pantry door. Fitments ...

FIELDING. Fitments.

> (*They laugh: look over at* KENDAL; *he re-examines the tools inside the parcel.*)

MORLEY. T'only bloody fitment thy needs, Kenny ... Nay, lad, thy weern't find wrapped up inside that box.

> (*They laugh;* FIELDING *sneezes.* KENDAL *begins to pack up his parcel.* HARRY *has gone out, having set the remaining jerseys. The door from the porch opens:* FENCHURCH, JAGGER *and* TREVOR *come in.*)

FENCHURCH *is a neatly groomed man, small, almost dainty; wears a suit beneath a belted raincoat. He carries a small hold-all in which he keeps his boots: self-contained, perhaps even at times a vicious man.*

JAGGER *is of medium height, but sturdy. He wears an overcoat, with an upturned collar, and carries a newspaper: perky, rather officious, cocky.*

TREVOR *is a studious-looking man; wears glasses, is fairly sturdily built. Quiet, level-headed: a schoolmaster.*)

FIELDING. Fenny.

MORLEY. Fenchurch.

FENCHURCH. Na, lad.

JAGGER. Come up in old Fenny's bloody car ... (*To* LUKE) By God: nearly needed thee there, Lukey ... Blind as a bloody bat is yon ... Old feller crossing the bleedin' road: tips him up the arse with his bloody bumper.

FENCHURCH. He started coming backwards. In't that right. then, Trevor?

TREVOR. Aye. He seemed to.

LUKE. Did he get your name?

JAGGER. Old Fenny gets out of the bleedin' car ... How much did you give him?

FENCHURCH. A bloody fiver.

TREVOR. A ten-bob note.

JAGGER. The bloody miser ...

TREVOR. Bends down, tha knows ...

JAGGER. He picks him up ...

TREVOR. Dusts down his coat ...

JAGGER. Asks him how he was ... Is that right? That's all you gave him?

FENCHURCH. Gone to his bloody head if I'd have given him any more.

(*They laugh.*)

TREVOR (*instructional*). You told him who you were, though, Fen.

JAGGER. Offered him his bloody autograph.

(*They laugh.*)

MORLEY. I went up to Fenny's one bloody night ... He said, 'I won't give you my address ... just mention my name to anyone you see ... ' Stopped a bobby at the end of his bloody road: 'Could you tell me where Gordon Fenchurch lives? Plays on the wing for the bloody City?' 'Who?' he said. '*Who?*' 'Fenchurch.' 'Fenchurch? Never heard of him.'

(*They laugh.* FENCHURCH, *taking no notice of this, has merely got out his boots and begun to examine them.*

HARRY *has come in with boots.*)

JAGGER. Ay up, ay up. Ay up. He's here. Look what the bloody ragman's brought.

(WALSH *comes in: a large, somewhat commanding figure. He wears a dark suit with a large carnation in the buttonhole. He enters from the offices, pausing in the door. He's smoking a cigar. His age, thirty-five to forty. Stout, fairly weather-beaten. There are cries and mocking shouts at his appearance:* '*Ay up, ay up, Walshy, then.' 'What's this?'*)

WALSH. And er ... who are all these bloody layabouts in here?

FIELDING. The bloody workers, lad. Don't you worry.

WALSH. I hope the floor's been swept then, Harry ... Keep them bloody microbes off my chair ... (*Comes in.*) Toe-caps polished with *equal* brightness, Harry ... (*To* JAGGER) I hate to find one toe-cap brighter than the next.

JAGGER. White laces.

WALSH. White laces.

(HARRY *has set the boots down. Goes out.*)

MORLEY. Where you been, then, Walshy?

WALSH. Been?

FIELDING. Been up in the bloody offices, have you? (*Gestures overhead.*)

WALSH. ... Popped up. Saw the managing director. Inquired about the pitch ... Asked him if they could *heat it up* ... thaw out one or two little bumps I noticed. Sir Frederick's going round now with a box of matches ... applying a drop of heat in all the appropriate places ... Should be nice and soft by the time you run out theer.

FIELDING. Thy's not coming with us, then?

WALSH. Nay, not for bloody me to tell ...

MORLEY. It's up to more important folk than Walsh ...

WALSH. Not more important ... more influential ... (*Watching* TREVOR) Saw you last week with one of your classes, Trev ... Where wa're it, now, then. Let me think ...

TREVOR. Don't know.

WALSH. Quite close to the Municipal Park ... (*Winks to* JAGGER.) By God, some of the girls in that bloody school ... how old are they, Trev?

TREVOR. Fourteen.

WALSH. Fourteen. Could have fooled me, old lad. Could have bloody well fooled me entirely. Old Trevor: guides them over the road, you know ... *by hand.*

FENCHURCH. Where have you been, then, Walshy?

WALSH (*conscious of his carnation quite suddenly, then cigar*). Wedding.

JAGGER. A wedding.

WALSH. Not mine ... Sister-in-law's as a matter of fact.

TREVOR. Sister-in-law?

WALSH. Married to me brother. Just got married a second time. Poor lass ... Had to come away. Just got going ... T'other bloody team's arrived ...

JAGGER. Seen the bus? (*Gestures size, etc.*)

WALSH. Ran over me bloody foot as near as not ... 'Be thy bloody head next, Walsh' ... Said it from the bloody

20

window! ... Said, 'Bloody well get out theer and tell me
then' ... gesturing at the field behind.

(*They laugh.*)

Load o' bloody pansies. Tell it at a glance ... Off back
theer, as a matter of fact. Going to give a dance ... Thy's
invited, Jagger, lad. Kitted out ... Anybody else fancy a
dance tonight? Champagne ... (*Belches: holds stomach.*) I'll
be bloody ill if I drink owt else ...

LUKE. Thy doesn't want to let old Sandford hear you.

WALSH. Sandford. Sandford ... Drop me from this team, old
lad ... I'd gi'e him half o' what I earned.

LUKE. One week's dropped wages and he's round here in a
bloody flash.

WALSH. There was some skirt at that bloody wedding,
Jagger ... (*To* TREVOR) Steam thy bloody glasses up, old
lad.

JAGGER. You're forgetting now ... Trevor here's already
married.

WALSH. She coming to watch, then, Trev, old lad?

TREVOR. Don't think so. No.

WALSH. Never comes to watch. His wife ... A university
degree ... what wa're it in?

TREVOR. Economics.

WALSH. Economics ... (*To* FENCHURCH) How do you fancy
being wed to that?

(FENCHURCH *goes off through bath entrance.*)

JAGGER. Wouldn't mind being married to bloody ought,
wouldn't Fenny.

FIELDING. Tarts: should see the bloody ones he has.

(WALSH *has warmed his hands, rubbing.*)

WALSH. Kenny: how's thy wife keeping, then, old lad?

KENDAL. All right.

WALSH (*looking in the parcel*). Bought her a do-it-yourself kit,
have you?

KENDAL. Bought it for meself.

MORLEY. Going to put up one or two shelves and cupboards ... and what was that, now?

FIELDING. Fitments.

MORLEY. Fitments.

WALSH. By Christ, you want to be careful theer, old lad ... Ask old Jaggers. He's very keen on fitments.

LUKE. Come on, Walsh. You'll be bloody well still talking theer when it's time to be going out ... Morley: let's have a bloody look, old lad.

(HARRY *has come in with last boots.*

LUKE *has strapped up* PATSY's *shoulder.* PATSY *goes back to finish changing, easing his shoulder.*

MORLEY *comes over to the bench: sits down on it, half-lying, his legs stretched out.* LUKE *examines his ankle: massages with oil; starts to strap it.*

WALSH *boxes with* JAGGER, *then goes over to his peg.*)

WALSH. Sithee, Harry: I hope thy's warmed up Patsy's jersey.

MORLEY. Don't want him catching any colds outside ...

(*They laugh.* PATSY *has taken his jersey over to the fire to warm, holding it in front of him.*)

FENCHURCH (*returning*). Seen that bloody bog?

JAGGER. Won't catch Sir Frederick, now, in theer.

FENCHURCH. Thy wants to get it seen to, Harry.

HARRY. Has been seen to ...

WALSH. Alus go afore I come. Drop off at the bloody peek-a-boo ... now what's it called?

JAGGER. Nude-arama.

WALSH. Best pair o' bogs this side o' town ... Lukey, gi'e us a rub, will you, when I'm ready?

(*Slaps* LUKE's *shoulder then backs up to the fire, elbowing* PATSY *aside.*

LUKE *is strapping* MORLEY's *ankle.*)

MORLEY. God Christ ... go bloody steady. (*Winces.*)

LUKE. Does it hurt?

MORLEY. Too tight.

TREVOR (*watching*). Don't worry. It'll slacken off.

    (HARRY *goes off.*)

FIELDING (*calling*). What've you got on this afternoon, then, Jagger?

JAGGER (*looking at his paper*). A fiver.

FIELDING. What's that, then?

JAGGER. Two-thirty.

WALSH. Bloody Albatross.

JAGGER. You what?

WALSH. Seven to one.

JAGGER. You've never.

WALSH. What you got, then?

JAGGER. Little Nell.

    (HARRY *has come in with shoulder-pads and tie-ups.*)

WALSH. Little Nell. Tripped over its bloody nose-bag ... now, when wa're it ...

JAGGER. See thy hosses home, old lad.

WALSH. About ten hours after the bloody start.

    (*They laugh.*

    HARRY *is taking shoulder-pads to* JAGGER, PATSY, FENCHURCH, *dropping the tie-ups for the stockings on the floor, then taking the last of the shoulder-pads to Stringer's peg.* SANDFORD *has come in through the office door. He's a man of about forty, medium build; he wears an overcoat, which is now open, and carries a programme with one or two papers clipped to a pen. Stands for a moment in the door, sniffing. The others notice him but make no comment, almost as if he wasn't there.*)

SANDFORD. I can smell cigar smoke ... (*Looks round.*) Has somebody been smoking bloody cigars?

    (WALSH, *back to the fire, is holding his behind him.*)

JAGGER. It's Harry, Mr Sandford. He's got one here.

WALSH. That's not a bloody cigar he's got, old lad.

HARRY. I don't smoke. It's not me. Don't worry.

(*They laugh.*)

MORLEY. Come on, now, Harry. What's thy bloody got?

(HARRY *avoids them as* JAGGER *sets at him. Goes.*)

SANDFORD (*to* WALSH). Is it you, Ken?

WALSH. Me?

FIELDING. Come on, now, bloody Walsh. Own up.

WALSH. Wheer would I get a bloody cigar? (*Puts the cigar in his mouth; approaches* SANDFORD.) I was bloody well stopped five quid this week. Thy never telled me ... What's it for, then, Sandy?

SANDFORD. Bloody language.

WALSH. Language?

SANDFORD. Referee's report ... Thy wants to take that out.

WALSH. Out? (*Puffs.*)

(SANDFORD *removes it; carefully stubs it out.*)

SANDFORD. You can have it back when you're bloody well dressed and ready to go home ... If you want the report you can read it in the office.

WALSH. Trevor: exert thy bloody authority, lad. Players' representative. Get up in that office ... (*To* SANDFORD) If there's any been bloody well smoked I shall bloody well charge thee: don't thee bloody worry ... Here, now: let's have it bloody back.

(*Takes it out of* SANDFORD'*s pocket, takes* SANDFORD'*s pencil, marks the cigar.*

*They laugh.*)

Warned you. Comes bloody expensive, lad, does that.

(*Puts cigar back. Goes over to bench to change.*)

SANDFORD (*to* MORLEY). How's thy ankle?

MORLEY. All right. Bit stiff.

LUKE (*to* SANDFORD). It'll ease up. Don't worry.

SANDFORD. Patsy: how's thy shoulder?

PATSY. All right. (*Eases it, winces.*) Strapped it up. (*He's now put on a pair of shoulder-pads and is getting ready to pull on his jersey.*)

> (*The others are now in the early stages of getting changed, though* WALSH *has made no progress and doesn't intend to, and* FENCHURCH *and* JAGGER *are reading the racing page of the paper, still dressed.*
>
> HARRY *has come in. Puts down more tie-ups; wanders round picking up pieces from the floor, trying to keep the room tidy. The door from the porch opens and* COPLEY *comes in, limping, barging against the door. He's followed in by* STRINGER. COPLEY *is a stocky, muscular man; simple, good-humoured, straightforward.* STRINGER *is tall and slim; aloof, with little interest in any of the others. He goes straight to his peg and checks his kit; nods briefly to the others as he crosses.* COPLEY *staggers to the fire.*)

COPLEY. God ... It's like a bloody ice-rink out theer ... Christ ... (*Pulls up his trouser-leg.*)

SANDFORD. Are you all right ...

COPLEY. Just look at that.

WALSH. Blood. Mr Sandford ... Mr Sandford. Blood.

COPLEY. You want to get some salt down, Harry ... (*To* SANDFORD) Thy'll have a bloody accident out theer afore tonight.

> (LUKE *crosses over to have a look as well. He and* SANDFORD *gaze down at* COPLEY's *knee.*)

JAGGER. You all right, then, Stringer?

STRINGER. Aye.

JAGGER. No cuts and bruises.

STRINGER. No.

MORLEY. Get nowt out of Stringer. In't that right, then, Jack?

> (STRINGER *doesn't answer.*)

LUKE. Well, I can't see a mark.

COPLEY. Could'a sworn it wa' bloody cut.

WALSH. Wants to cry off there, Mr Sandford. (*To* COPLEY)
Seen the bloody pitch thy has.

COPLEY. Piss off.

>    (*They laugh.*)

SANDFORD (*to* STRINGER). Jack, then. You all right?

STRINGER. Aye.

SANDFORD. Who else is there?

JAGGER. There's bloody Owens: saw him walking up.

FENCHURCH. Stopped to give him a bloody lift.

JAGGER. Said he was warming up.

WALSH. Warming up!

>    (*Blows raspberry. They laugh.*)

JAGGER. Silly prick.

SANDFORD (*to* TREVOR). You all right?

TREVOR. Thanks.

SANDFORD. Saw your wife the other night.

TREVOR. So she said.

WALSH. Ay, ay. Ay, ay ...

FENCHURCH. Heard that.

WALSH. Bloody Sandford ...

JAGGER. Coach old Trevor, Sandy, not his wife.

SANDFORD. It was a meeting in the Town Hall, as a matter of
fact.

WALSH. Sithee—Harry: pricked up his bloody ears at that.

FIELDING. What was the meeting about, then, Mr Sandford?

SANDFORD. Just a meeting.

FENCHURCH. Town Hall, now: that's a draughty bloody
place, is that.

>    (*They laugh.*
>
>    HARRY *goes out.*)

WALSH. Come on, now, Trevor. What's it all about?

TREVOR. Better ask Mr Sandford.

WALSH. He'll have no idea. Can't spell his name for a bloody start.

> (*They laugh.*
> *The door opens:* ATKINSON *comes in, followed by* SPENCER, CLEGG *and* MOORE.)

ATKINSON. Jesus! Jesus! Lads! Look out! (*Crosses, rubbing hands, to fire.*)

CLEGG. How do. How do. (*Follows him over to the fire, rubbing hands.*) By God, but it's bloody freezing.

> (ATKINSON *is a tall, big-boned man, erect, easy-going. He wears a threequarter-length jacket and flat cap.*
> CLEGG *is a square, stocky, fairly small man, bare-headed, in an overcoat and scarf.*)

MORLEY. Here you are, then, Cleggy. I've gotten the spot just here, if you want to warm your hands.

> (*They laugh.*
> SPENCER *and* MOORE *are much younger men. They come in, nervous, hands in pockets.*)

How's young Billy keeping, then?

SPENCER. All right.

WALSH. Been looking after him, have you, Frank?

MOORE. Be keeping a bloody eye on thee, then, Walsh.

FIELDING. Babes in the bloody wood, are yon.

ATKINSON. Here, then. I hear that the bloody game's been cancelled.

FENCHURCH. Cancelled?

COPLEY. Cancelled?

FENCHURCH. Cancelled?

MORLEY. Here, then, Bryan: who told you that?

ATKINSON. A little bird ...

CLEGG. We were coming up ...

ATKINSON. Came over ...

CLEGG. Whispered in his ear ...

JAGGER. Give over ...

FENCHURCH. Piss off.

COPLEY. Rotten bloody luck.

(ATKINSON *and* SPENCER *laugh.*)

Sit on their bloody backsides up yonder.

MORLEY. Give ought, now, to have me hands in Sir Frederick's bloody pockets …

WALSH. Dirty bloody sod …

MORLEY. Warming. Warming …

WALSH. Come on, now, Sandy. Let it out. (*To* ATKINSON *and* CLEGG) He's been having it off here, now, with Trevor's wife.

TREVOR. All right, Walsh.

LUKE. We've had enough of that.

SANDFORD. The meeting … was about … a municipal centre.

JAGGER. A municipal what?

FENCHURCH. Centre.

CLEGG. Centre.

SANDFORD. There you are. I could have telled you.

WALSH. Sir Frederick bloody Thornton.

JAGGER. What?

WALSH. Going to build it …

SANDFORD. That's right.

WALSH. Votes for it on the bloody council …

JAGGER. Puts in his tender …

SANDFORD. He's not even on the council.

CLEGG. All his bloody mates are, though.

SANDFORD. He asked me to attend, as a matter of fact. There are more important things in life than bloody football.

CLEGG. Not today there isn't.

SANDFORD. Not today there, John, you're right … Now, then, Frank: are you all right?

MOORE. Aye.

SANDFORD. Billy?

SPENCER. Aye. I'm fine.

SANDFORD. Right. Let's have you bloody well stripped off ...
None of you seen Clifford Owens, have you?

MOORE. No.

SPENCER. No ...

SANDFORD (*looking at watch*). By God: he's cutting it bloody
fine.

    (*With varying speeds, they've all started stripping off.*
    HARRY *has distributed all the kit and checked it.*
    LUKE, *after strapping* MORLEY's *ankle, has started strapping*
    STRINGER's *body, wrapping it round and round with tape,*
    STRINGER *standing by the table, arms held out.*)

WALSH (*to* SANDFORD). Here, then ... Get a bit of stuff on ...
Let's see you do some bloody work.

    (WALSH *lies down on the table.*
    LUKE *has put his various medicine bottles from his bag by the*
    *table.*
    SANDFORD *opens one, pours oil onto the palm of his hand*
    *and starts to rub* WALSH *down.*)

KENDAL. Is there anywhere I can keep this, Lukey?

COPLEY. What you got in there, Kenny?

MORLEY. He's bought an electric tool-kit, Luke.

KENDAL. Aye.

FIELDING. Show him it, Kenny. Let him have a look.

KENDAL. Drill ... electric polisher ... sandpaper ... electric saw
... Do owt with that.

    (*Shows it to* COPLEY. FENCHURCH *and* JAGGER *look at it*
    *as well.*)

COPLEY. We better tek it with us yonder, Kenny. Bloody well
mek use o' that today.

    (*They laugh.*)

STRINGER. I've got one of those at home.

KENDAL. Oh?

STRINGER. Aye.

JAGGER (*winking at the others*). Is that right, then, Jack?

STRINGER. Get through a lot o' work wi' that.

JAGGER. Such as?

KENDAL. Bookcases.

JAGGER. Bookcases?

STRINGER. I've made one or two toys, an' all.

KENDAL. Any amount of things.

STRINGER. That's right.

FENCHURCH. Who did you give the toys to, Jack?

STRINGER. What?

JAGGER. Toys.

STRINGER. Neighbour's lad ...

FENCHURCH. Your mother fancies you, then, with one of those?

STRINGER. She doesn't mind.

COPLEY. You ought to get together here with Ken.

ATKINSON. Bloody main stand could do with a few repairs.
(*They laugh.*)

WALSH. Take no bloody notice, Jack ... If thy's got an electric tool-kit, keep it to thysen ... Here, then, Sandy ... lower ... lower!
(*They laugh.*)
By God, I could do that better, I think, mesen.

LUKE. Kenny: leave it with me, old lad. I'll keep an eye on it ... Anybody else now? Fieldy: how's thy eye?

FIELDING. Be all right. A spot of bloody grease.

LUKE (*to* COPLEY). Barry. Let's have your bloody back, old lad. (*Gets out more bandage.*)

(STRINGER *and* FENCHURCH *have put on shoulder-pads.* PATSY, *changed and ready, crosses to the mirror to comb his hair and examine himself; gets out piece of gum, adjusts socks, etc.*
*The tin of grease stands on the second table by the wall. After the players have stripped, got on their shorts, they dip in the tin and grease up: legs, arms, shoulders, neck, ears.*

*The stockings they fasten with the tie-ups* HARRY *has dropped on the floor. A slight air of expectation has begun to filter through the room: players rubbing limbs, rubbing hands together, shaking fingers, flexing; tense.*

*At this point* CROSBY *comes in. He's dressed in a track-suit and enters from the office. A stocky, gnarled figure, late forties or fifties.*)

CROSBY. Come on ... come on ... half ready ... The other team are changed already ...

(*Calls of 'Ah, give over,' 'Get lost,' 'Silly sods,' etc.*)

SANDFORD. Clifford hasn't come yet, Danny.

CROSBY. He's upstairs.

WALSH. Upstairs?

CROSBY (*looking round at the others, on tip-toe, checking those present*). Bill? Billy?

SPENCER (*coming out*). Aye ... I'm here.

CROSBY. Frank?

MOORE. Aye ... I'm here.

CROSBY. On the bench today, then, lads.

(SANDFORD *slaps* WALSH *who gets up to finish changing.* CLEGG *lies down to be massaged.*

LUKE *is strapping* COPLEY's *body with crepe bandage and strips of plaster.*)

WALSH. What's old Owens doing upstairs?

CROSBY. Minding his own bloody business, lad.

CLEGG. Having a word with His Highness, is he?

CROSBY. Patsy. How's your shoulder, lad?

PATSY. All right ... stiff ... (*Eases it up and down in illustration.*)

CROSBY. Fieldy. How's thy eye?

FIELDING. All right.

CROSBY (*suddenly sniffing*). Bloody cigars. Who the hell's been smoking?

LUKE. What?

CROSBY. Not ten minutes afore a bloody match. Come on.

SANDFORD. Oh ... aye ... here ...

CROSBY. You know the bloody rule in here, then, Sandy?

SANDFORD. Yes. Aye. Sorry. Put it out.

LUKE. Is Clifford changed, then, Danny?

CROSBY (*distracted*). What?

LUKE. Need a rub, or strapping up, or ought?

CROSBY. Changed ... He's gotten changed already.

WALSH. Bloody well up theer? By God, then. Bridal bloody suite is that.

CROSBY. Jack? All right, then, are you?

STRINGER. Fine. Aye ... Fine. All right.

CROSBY. Trevor?

TREVOR. All right.

CROSBY. Bloody well hard out theer. When you put 'em down ... knock 'em bleeding hard.

WALSH. And what's Owens bloody well been up to? Arranging a bloody transfer, is he? Or asking for a rise?
  (*They laugh.*)

CROSBY (*reading from a list*). Harrison's on the wing this afternoon, Patsy. Alus goes off his left foot, lad.

PATSY. Aye. Right. (*Rubs arms, legs, etc.*)
  (*He and* CLEGG *laugh.*)

CROSBY. Scrum-half: new. Barry: when you catch him knock him bloody hard ... Morley?

MORLEY. Aye!

CROSBY. Same with you. Get round. Let him know you're theer ... Same goes for you, Bryan.

ATKINSON. Aye.

CROSBY. Kenny ... Let's see you bloody well go right across.

MORLEY. He's brought something to show you here, Mr Crosby.

CROSBY. What?

MORLEY. Kenny ... Show him your bloody outfit, Ken.

KENDAL (*after a certain hesitation*). Piss off!
  (*They laugh.*)

WALSH. You tell him, Kenny, lad. That's right.

JAGGER (*to* KENDAL). Anybody gets in thy road ... (*Smacks his fist against his hand.*)

CLEGG. Ne'er know which is bloody harder. Ground out yon or Kenny's loaf.
(*They laugh.*)

CROSBY. Jack ... Jagger ...

STRINGER. Aye.

JAGGER. Aye ...

CROSBY. Remember what we said. Keep together ... don't be waiting theer for Trev ... If Jack goes right, then you go with him ... Trevor: have you heard that, lad?

TREVOR. Aye.

CROSBY. Use your bloody eyes ... John?

CLEGG. Aye?

CROSBY. Let's have a bit of bloody service, lad.

CLEGG. Cliff been complaining, has he?

CROSBY. Complained about bloody nowt. It's me who's been complaining ... Michaelmas bloody Morley ... when you get that bloody ball ... remember ... don't toss it o'er your bloody head.

WALSH. Who's refereeing then, old lad?

CROSBY. Tallon.
(*Groans and cries.*)

JAGGER. Brought his bloody white stick, then, has he?

FENCHURCH. Got his bloody guide-dog, then?

CROSBY (*undisturbed; to* COPLEY). Watch your putting in near your own line, Barry ... No fists. No bloody feet. Remember ... But when you hit them. Hit them bleeding hard. (*Looks at his watch.*) There's some gum. Walshy: how's thy back?

WALSH. She told me, Danny, she'd never seen ought like it.
(*They laugh.*
CROSBY *drops the packets of chewing-gum on the table.*

*Goes over to talk to the players separately, helping them
with jerseys, boots, etc.*
CLEGG *gets up from the table.* JAGGER *comes to have his leg
massaged by* SANDFORD.
*Faint military music can be heard from outside, and the low
murmur of a crowd.*
FIELDING *comes over to have his eye examined by* LUKE: *he
greases it over.* FIELDING *goes back.)*

CROSBY. Any valuables: let me have 'em ... Any watches,
ear-rings, anklets, cigarettes ...

ALL. Give over. Not bloody likely. Safer to chuck 'em out
o' bloody winder ...

(*Laughter.* CROSBY, LUKE *and* SANDFORD *take valuables
and put them in their pockets.*

OWENS *comes in through the office door, dressed in a
track-suit: bright red with* CITY *on the back; underneath
he's already changed. Medium build, unassuming, bright,
about thirty to thirty-two years old, he's rubbing his hands
together, cheerful. A shy man, perhaps, but now a little
perky.*)

OWENS. All right, then. Are we ready?

JAGGER. Sod off.

FENCHURCH. Give over.

FIELDING. Where you been?

(*Cries and shouts.*

HARRY *has come in with track-suits; gives them to* MOORE
*to give out. Goes out.*)

OWENS. Told me upstairs you were fit and ready. 'Just need
you, Cliff,' they said, 'to lead them out.'

WALSH. And how's Sir Frederick keeping, then?

OWENS. Asked me to come up a little early.

ALL. Ay, ay. Ay, ay. What's that? Give over.

OWENS. Fill him in on the tactics we intend to use today.

SANDFORD. That's right.

JAGGER. What tactics are those, then, Clifford?

OWENS. Told him one or two hand signals he might look out for, Jag.

> (*They laugh.*
> *The players are picking up gum, tense, flexing. Occasionally one or other goes out through the bath entrance, returning a few moments later.*
> HARRY *has come in with buckets and bottles of water.*)

Freeze the eyeballs off a copper monkey, boy, today. By God ... (*Goes over to the fire.*) Could do with a bit more coal on, Harry.

SANDFORD. You want to keep away from that bloody fire ...

LUKE. Get cramp if you stand in front of that.

WALSH. Got cramp in one place, Luke, already.

> (*They laugh.*)

OWENS. Just watch the ball today, boy. Come floating over like a bloody bird.

WALSH. If you listened to half he said afore a bloody match you'd never get out on that bloody field ... Does it all, you know, inside his bloody head ... How many points do you give us, then, today?

OWENS. Sod all. You'll have to bloody earn 'em, lad.

SANDFORD. That's the bloody way to talk.

CROSBY. Harry ... where's the bloody resin board, old lad?

JAGGER. Let's have a bloody ball, an' all.

> (*Roar off of the crowd.*
> HARRY *goes off through bath entrance.*)

MORLEY. What bonus are we on today, then, Danny?

CROSBY. All 'bonus thy'll get, lad, you'll find on t'end o' my bloody boot ... Now come on, come on, then, lads. Get busy ...

> (CROSBY *is moving amongst the players; now all of them are almost ready: moving over to the mirror, combing hair, straightening collars, tightening boots, chewing, greasing*

*ears, emptying coat pockets of wallets, etc., and handing them to* CROSBY, SANDFORD *or* LUKE.

TALLON *comes in: a soldierly man of about forty, dressed in black referee's shorts and shirt.*)

TALLON. You all ready, then, in here?

SANDFORD. Aye. Come in, Mr Tallon. We're all ready, then. All set.

TALLON. Good day for it.

CROSBY. Aye. Take away a bit o' frost.

TALLON. Right. I'll have a look. Make sure that nobody's harbouring any weapons.

(*A couple of players laugh.*

TALLON *goes round to each player, examines his hands for rings, his boots for protruding studs; feels their bodies for any belts, buckles or protruding pads. He does it quickly; each player nods in greeting; one or two remain aloof.*

*As* TALLON *goes round,* HARRY *comes back with the resin board and two rugby balls; sets the board on the table against the wall. The players take the balls, feel them, pass them round, lightly, casual.*

HARRY *moves off, to the bath entrance. He takes the coal-bucket with him.*

OWENS *takes off his track-suit to several whistles; exchanges greetings, formally, with* TALLON.

*After each player's been examined he goes over to the resin board, rubs his hands in the resin, tries the ball.*

SPENCER *and* MOORE *have pulled on red track-suits over their playing-gear.*)

WALSH. By God, I could do with wekening up ... Lukey: where's thy bloody phials?

OWENS. Off out tonight, then, Walshy, lad?

WALSH. I am. Two arms, two legs, one head. If you pass the bloody ball mek sure I'm bloody looking.

(*They laugh.*)

OWENS. Ton o' rock there, Walshy, lad.

WALSH. Second bloody half ... where wa're it? ... 'Walshy!
Walshy! Walshy!' ... Passes ... Fastening me bloody boot,
what else.

JAGGER. Never looks.

WALSH. Came down like a ton o' bloody lead.

(*They laugh.*

*LUKE has got out a tin of ammonia phials. The players
take them, sniff, coughing, flinging back their heads; pass
them on to the others. Several of the backs don't bother.*
WALSH *takes his, breathes deeply up either nostril: no
effect.*)

JAGGER. Shove a can o' coal-gas up theer: wouldn't make
much bloody difference.

WALSH. Mr Tallon! Mr Tallon! You haven't inspected me,
Mr Tallon!

(*They laugh.* TALLON *comes over, finishing off.*)

TALLON. All right, then, Walshy. Let's have a look.

(WALSH, *arms raised, submits ponderously to* TALLON's
*inspection.*)

WALSH. Count 'em! Count 'em! Don't just bloody look.

(*The players laugh.*

TALLON *finishes, goes over to the door.*)

TALLON (*to the room*). Remember ... keep it clean ... play fair.
Have a good game, lads. Play to the whistle.

ALL. Aye. All right.

TALLON. All right, then, lads. I'll see you. May the best team
win. Good luck.

(*An electric bell rings as* TALLON *goes out.*)

CROSBY. Okay. Five minutes ... Forr'ads. Let's have you ...
Billy? Frank? You ready?

MOORE. Aye.

SPENCER. Aye ...

CROSBY. Over here, then. O'd these up.

(CLEGG *raises his arms;* WALSH *and* FIELDING *lock in on either side, casual, not much effort.*

ATKINSON *and* KENDAL *bind together and put their heads in-between the three in front.*)

FIELDING. Ger off. Ger off!

WALSH. A bit lower there, then, Kenny ... Lovely. Beautiful.

CLEGG. Just right.

(*They laugh.*)

CROSBY (*holding the forwards with* SPENCER *and* MOORE). All right. All right.

(MORLEY *leans on* ATKINSON *and* KENDAL, *then, at* CROSBY'*s signal, puts his head between them as they scrum down.*

SPENCER, MOORE *and* CROSBY *are linked together.*)

Let's have a ball ... Cliff ... Barry ... Number four: first clear scrum we get: either side ... (*Takes the ball* SANDFORD'*s brought him.*) Our possession, theirs ... Clifford ... Jagger ... Jack ... that's right.

(*The rest of the players take up positions behind:* COPLEY *immediately behind, then* OWENS, *then* STRINGER, JAGGER *and* PATSY *on one side,* FENCHURCH *on the other.* TREVOR *stands at the back.*)

Right, then? Our ball, then ...

(CROSBY *puts the ball in at* CLEGG'*s feet. It's knocked back through the scrum to* COPLEY; *then it's passed, hand to hand, slowly, almost formally, out to* PATSY. *As each player passes it, he falls back; the scrum breaks up, falls back to make a line going back diagonally and ending with* FENCHURCH.)

WALSH. From me. To you ...

(*Laughter.*)

CROSBY. All right. All right.

(*When the ball reaches* PATSY *he passes it back: to* JAGGER, *to* STRINGER, *to* OWENS, *to* COPLEY, *each calling the*

*Christian name of the one who hands it on, until it reaches* FENCHURCH.)

WALSH. Run, Fenny! Run!

JAGGER. Go on. Go on! It'll be t'on'y bloody chance thy has. (*They laugh.*)

WALSH. I never know whether it's bloody speed or fear with Fenny ... The sound of a pair of bloody feet behind.

(WALSH *catches his backside. They laugh.*)

CROSBY. All right. All right ... Trev: number six.

SANDFORD. Come up on your positions, lads: remember that.

(*They get down as before, though this time* MORLEY *stands out and takes* COPLEY's *place.* COPLEY *falls back;* OWENS *falls back behind him.* JAGGER *and* PATSY *stand on one side of* OWENS, STRINGER *and* FENCHURCH *on the other;* TREVOR *stands immediately behind him.*)

CROSBY. Remember: first time up ... Cliff'll give his signal ... our head; their put in ... doesn't matter ...

(CROSBY *puts the ball in the scrum as before. The forwards play it back between their feet.* MORLEY *takes it, turns, passes it back to* COPLEY; COPLEY *passes it back to* OWENS, OWENS *to* TREVOR, *who runs and mimes a drop kick.*)

JAGGER. Pow!

(HARRY *has come in with coal-bucket.*)

WALSH. Now thy's sure thy won't want thy glasses, Trev? (*One or two laugh.*)

TREVOR. Just about.

WALSH. If you can't see the posts just give a shout. (*They laugh.*)

JAGGER. Walshy here'll move 'em up. (*Laughter.*)

CROSBY. All right. All right. I'll say nowt else ...

(*The door from the office has already opened.*

THORNTON *comes in: tall, dressed in a fur-collared overcoat. A well-preserved man of about fifty.*

*He's accompanied by* MACKENDRICK, *a flush-faced man of about sixty. He wears an overcoat, a scarf and a dark hat.*)

THORNTON. Hope I'm not intruding, Danny.

CROSBY. No, no. Not at all.

THORNTON. Thought I'd have a word.

SANDFORD. That's right.

(SANDFORD *gestures at the players. They move round in a half-circle as* THORNTON *crosses to the centre.*)

THORNTON. Chilly in here. That fire could do with a spot of stoking ...

MACKENDRICK. Harry ... spot o' coal on that.

HARRY. Aye ... Right ... (*Mends the fire.*)

THORNTON. Just to wish you good luck, lads.

PLAYERS. Thanks ...

THORNTON. Fair play, tha knows, has always had its just rewards.

SANDFORD. Aye ...

THORNTON. Go out ... play like I know you can ... there'll not be one man disappointed ... Now, then. Any grunts and groans? Any complaints? No suggestions? (*Looks round.*)

JAGGER. No ...

FENCHURCH. No, Sir Frederick ...

CROSBY. No.

SANDFORD. No, Sir Frederick ...

THORNTON. Right, then ... Mr Mackendrick here'll be in his office, afterwards ... if there's anything you want, just let him know ... Good luck. Play fair. May the best team win ... Cliff. Good luck.

OWENS. Thanks. (*Shakes his hand.*)

MACKENDRICK. Good luck, Cliff ... Good luck, lads ...

PLAYERS. Aye ... Thanks.

THORNTON. Danny.

CROSBY. Aye. Right ... Thanks.

THORNTON. Good luck, lads. See you later.

MACKENDRICK. Danny …

(THORNTON *waves, cheerily, and followed by* MAC-
KENDRICK, *goes.*
*Silence. Broken finally by* HARRY, *stoking fire.*
*Crowd roars off; fanfare music; the opposing team runs on.
A bell rings in the room.*)

CROSBY. Right, then, lads … Cliff? Ought you'd like to add?

OWENS. No. (*Shakes his head.*) Play well, lads …

PLAYERS. Aye …

(*The players, tense, nervous, start to line up prior to going
out.*
OWENS *takes the ball. He heads the column.*
*Crowd roars again; loudspeaker, indecipherable, announces
names.*)

WALSH. Harry: make sure that bloody bath is hot.

(HARRY *looks across. He nods his head.*)

Towel out, tha knows … me bloody undies ready …

CROSBY. Bloody Walsh … come on. Line up …

(*Groans, moans; the players line up behind* OWENS (6).)

TREVOR (1)
PATSY (2)
JAGGER (3)
STRINGER (4)
FENCHURCH (5)
COPLEY (7)
WALSH (8)
CLEGG (9)
FIELDING (10)
ATKINSON (11)
KENDAL (12)
MORLEY (13)

SPENCER (15) *and* MOORE (14), *in red track-suits with*
CITY *on the back, are helping* LUKE *and* SANDFORD

*collect the various pieces of equipment: spare kit, track-suits,*
*sponges, medical bag, spare ball, bucket.*
CROSBY *holds the door.*)

OWENS. Right, then?

ALL. Right. Ready. Let's get off. (*Belches, groans.*)

CROSBY. Good luck, Trev ... good luck, lad ... good luck ...
Good luck, Mic ...

> (*He pats each player's back as they move out. Moments*
> *after* OWENS *has gone there's a great roar outside.*
>
> CROSBY *sees the team out, then* SPENCER *and* MOORE *in*
> *track-suits, then* LUKE *and* SANDFORD. *He looks round,*
> *then he goes, closing the door.*
>
> *The roar grows louder. Music.*
>
> HARRY *comes in, wanders round, looks at the floor for*
> *anything that's been dropped, picks up odd tapes, phials.*
> *Goes to the fire; puts on another piece of coal, stands by*
> *it, still. The crowd roar grows louder.*
>
> *Then, slowly, lights and sound fade.*)

# ACT TWO

*The same. About thirty-five minutes later.*

*The dressing-room is empty, the light switched off. There's a faint glow from the fire.*

*The roar off of the crowd: rising to a crescendo, fading.*

*The door from the porch opens.* THORNTON *enters, rubbing his hands, followed by* MACKENDRICK.

THORNTON. By God ... (*Gasps, shudders, stumbling round.*) Where's the light switch?

MACKENDRICK. Here ...
    (*Light switched on.*)

THORNTON. How much longer?

MACKENDRICK (*looks at his watch*). Twelve ... fifteen minutes.

THORNTON. Could do with some heating in that bloody box ... either that or we watch it from the office. (*Crosses to the fire and warms his hands.*) Anybody in here, is there?

MACKENDRICK (*looks into the bath entrance*). Don't think so.

THORNTON. Got your flask?

MACKENDRICK. Empty. (*Shows him.*)

THORNTON (*rubbing his hands*). Send up to the office.

MACKENDRICK (*calls through the bath entrance*). Harry! (*Listens: no answer. Goes to office entrance.*)

THORNTON. You go, Mac ... He'll be up in the bloody canteen, that lad. (*Has settled himself in the chair in front of the fire.*)
    (*The crowd roars off.*)

MACKENDRICK. Shan't be a second.

THORNTON. Second cabinet on the right: my office.

MACKENDRICK. Right. (*Hesitates, goes off through office door.*)

43

(THORNTON *settles himself in front of the fire. Crowd roars off. He raises his head, listens.*
*The roar dies. He leans forward, puts piece of coal on the fire.*
*Door bangs off; stamping of feet; coughs, growls, clearing of throat, sighs.*
HARRY *comes in from the bath entrance, muffled up: balaclava, scarf, cap, ex-army overcoat, gloves.*)

HARRY. Oh ... Oh ... (*On the way to the fire sees* THORNTON *and stops, about to go back.*)

THORNTON. That's all right. Come in, Harry ... Taking a breather.

HARRY. I just nipped up to the er ...

THORNTON. That's all right, lad.

HARRY. Cup o' tea.

THORNTON. Pull up a chair, lad. (*Moves his own over fractionally.*)
(HARRY *looks round. There's no other chair. He remains standing where he is.*)
Nowt like a coal fire. Hardly get it anywhere now, you know ... Synthetic bloody fuel. Like these plastic bloody chickens. Get nought that's bloody real no more.

HARRY (*sways from one foot to the other*). Aye ...

THORNTON. Water's hot, then, is it?

HARRY. What?

THORNTON. For the bath.

HARRY. Oh. Aye ... (*Pause.*) I've just stoked up.

THORNTON. I'd have given you a hand myself if I'd have known. By God, that box ... like ice ... (*Takes hands out of his gloves.*) Can't feel a thing.

HARRY. It comes fro' Russia.

THORNTON. What?

HARRY. The cold.

THORNTON. Oh ...

HARRY. East wind ... Blows from the Russian steppes.

THORNTON (*looks up*). More north-west today, I think.

HARRY. Over the Baltic ... Norway ...

> (THORNTON *has raised his hand. The crowd's roar rises; he listens.* HARRY *waits. The roar dies down.*)

THORNTON. Them, I think ... Score today, our lads: they'll raise the bloody roof.

HARRY. I've read it in a book.

THORNTON. What?

HARRY. The Russians ... when the wind blows to the west — spray it with a special gas.

THORNTON. Good God.

HARRY. Without anybody knowing ... Breathe it ... Take it in ... (*Breathes in.*) Slows down your mind ... (*Illustrates with limp arms and hands.*) Stops everybody thinking.

THORNTON. I think our lads've had a drop of that today. By God, I've never seen so many bloody knock-ons ... dropped passes ...

HARRY. I've been a workman all my life.

THORNTON. Oh ... Aye.

HARRY. I used to work in a brickyard afore I came up here.

THORNTON. It's a pity you're not back theer, Harry lad. Bloody bricks we get. Come to pieces in your bloody hand ... Had a house fall down the other day. Know what it was ... ? Bricks ... crumbled up ... Seen nothing like it ... Still ...

HARRY. Knew your place before. Now, there's everybody doing summat ... And nobody doing owt.

THORNTON. Still. Go with it, Harry.

HARRY. What ...

THORNTON. Can't go against your times ... (*Twists round.*) Sent Mac up for a bloody snifter ... Had time to mek the bloody stuff by now.

> (*Crowd's roar rises; reaches crescendo; dies. Booing.*)

Don't know why they do that job, you know. Refereeing.
Must have a stunted mentality, in my view. To go on
with a thing like that.

HARRY. Be all communist afore long.

THORNTON. Aye. (*Pokes fire.*) If the Chinese don't get here
afore.

HARRY. It's happening all the time. In the mind ... Come one
day, they'll just walk in. Take over ... There'll be nobody
strong enough to stop them. They'll have all been brain-
washed ... You can see it happening ...

THORNTON (*calls*). *Mac!* Takes that man a fortnight to
brew a cup of tea. Accountant ... He'll be up there now,
counting the bloody gate receipts. I don't think he's at all
interested in bloody football ... He's never slow, you
know, to tell us when we've made a bloody loss.

(*Banging outside.* MACKENDRICK *comes in with the bottle.*)
Thought you'd been swigging the bloody bottle.

MACKENDRICK. It wasn't in the cabinet ... I had to get it
from the bar ... Got to sign about four receipts ... Anybody gets a drink in this place they bloody well deserve it,
lad.

THORNTON. No glasses?

MACKENDRICK. Here. (*Takes two from his pocket.*)

THORNTON. Was that a score?

MACKENDRICK. Penalty. Missed.

THORNTON. Them? Or us.

MACKENDRICK. Seven, two. Them. It'll take some pulling
back ... Harry. (*Nods.*)

HARRY. Mr Mackendrick.

MACKENDRICK. Wrapped up for the weather, Harry.

HARRY. Aye.

THORNTON. Been telling me: comes from Russia.

MACKENDRICK. Russia.

THORNTON. Weather.

MACKENDRICK. Weather!

THORNTON. Might have bloody guessed ... (*To* HARRY) Got a cup, then, have you? Try a drop o' this.

HARRY. Don't drink. Thanks all the same, Sir Frederick.

THORNTON. Nay, no bloody titles here, old lad. Freddy six days o' the week. (*To* MACKENDRICK) Sir Frederick to the wife on Sundays.

(THORNTON *and* MACKENDRICK *laugh.*

THORNTON *drinks.*)

By God. Brings back a drop of life, does that.

MACKENDRICK (*drinks, gasps*). Grand ... Lovely.

(*Roar of the crowd, huge, prolonged. They listen.*)

THORNTON. Have a look. Go on. Quick. You've missed it ...

(MACKENDRICK *goes to the porch; disappears outside.*)

How do you think they compare to the old days, Harry?

HARRY. Players? ... Couldn't hold a bloody candle ... In them days they'd do a sixteen-hour shift, *then* come up and lake ... Nowadays: it's all machines ... and they're *still* bloody puffed when they come up o' Sat'days. Run round yon field a couple of times: finished. I've seen 'em laking afore with broken arms, legs broke ... shoulders ... Get a scratch today and they're in here, flat on their bloody backs: iodine, liniment, injections ... If they ever played a real team today they wouldn't last fifteen bloody seconds. That's my view. That's what I think of them today. Everywheer. There's not one of them could hold a candle to the past.

(*Roar and cheering from the crowd.* THORNTON *twists round and listens.*)

They'll wek up one morning and find it's all too late ...

(MACKENDRICK *comes back in.*)

MACKENDRICK. Scored.

THORNTON (*pleased*). Try?

MACKENDRICK. Converted.

THORNTON. Who wa're it?

MACKENDRICK. Morley.

THORNTON. By God. Bloody genius that lad.

(MACKENDRICK *pours a drink.*)

MACKENDRICK. Harry … ?

HARRY. No thanks, Mr Mackendrick.

THORNTON. Harry here's been enlightening me about the past … Nothing like the old days, Mac.

HARRY. Aye!

MACKENDRICK. Bloody bunkum.

THORNTON. What's that? (*Laughs: pleased.*)

MACKENDRICK. God Christ … If this place was like it was twenty years ago—and that's not *too* far back—you wouldn't find me here for a bloody start … As for fifty years ago. Primeval … Surprised at thee, then, Harry lad.

HARRY. Aye … (*Turns away.*)

MACKENDRICK. Have another snifter.

THORNTON. Thanks.

(MACKENDRICK *pours it in.*)

MACKENDRICK (*to* HARRY). I'd have thought thy'd see the difference, lad.

(HARRY *doesn't answer, turns away.*)

Washed i' bloody buckets, then … et dripping instead o' bloody meat … urinated by an hedge … God Christ, bloody houses were nobbut size o' this—seven kiddies, no bloody bath: no bed … fa'ther out o' work as much as not.

HARRY. There's many as living like that right now!

MACKENDRICK. Aye. And there's a damn sight more as not.

THORNTON. I never knew you had strong feelings, Mac.

MACKENDRICK. About one or two bloody things I have.

(*He pours himself another drink. A faint roar from the crowd.*)

I suppose you're more on his side, then?

THORNTON. Nay, I'm on nobody's bloody side, old lad … I

had a dream the other night ... I was telling Cliff afore
the match ... I came up here to watch a match ... looked
over at the tunnel ... know what I saw run out? (*Laughs.*)
Bloody robots. (*Laughs again.*) And up in the bloody
box were a couple of fellers, just like Danny, flicking
bloody switches ... twisting knobs. (*Laughs.*) I laugh now.
I wok up in a bloody sweat, I tell you.

> (*Roar from the crowd, applause.*
> *Noises off: boots, shouting.*)

Ay up. Ay up ... (*Springs up.*)

HARRY. You'll wake up one day ... I've telled you ... You'll
wek up one day ... You'll find it's bloody well too late.
(*Goes off through bath entrance.*)

MACKENDRICK. Aren't you staying to see them in?

THORNTON. I'll pop in in a couple of jiffies, lad ... You stay
and give 'em a bloody cheer ... (*Slaps his shoulder.*) Shan't
be long ... (*Calls through to bath entrance*) Harry ... I'll
pursue that argument another time. (*Nods, winks at*
MACKENDRICK, *then goes out smartly through the office door.*)

> (MACKENDRICK *moves the chair from in front of the fire*
> *just as the players start to come in.*
> FENCHURCH *comes in first, shaking his hand violently. He's*
> *followed by* LUKE *carrying his bag.*)

FENCHURCH. Jesus! Jesus! Bloody hell.

LUKE. Here ... Let's have a look. Come on.

JAGGER (*following him in*). It's nothing ... bloody nothing ...

FENCHURCH. Bloody studs, you see ... Just look!

> (*He holds it up, wincing, as* LUKE *takes it. He groans, cries*
> *out, as* LUKE *examines it.*
> *The others are beginning to flood in: stained jerseys, gasping,*
> *bruised, exhausted.*
> HARRY *brings in two bottles of water; the players take*
> *swigs from them and spit out into* LUKE'S *bucket which*
> MOORE *has carried in.*)

LUKE. Nothing broken. It'll be all right.

SANDFORD. Do you want me to bind it for you, then?

FENCHURCH. No, no. No ... No.

JAGGER. Can't hold the ball with a bandage on.

COPLEY. Have you off to hospital, Fenny, lad. Match o'er: don't worry. Operation. Have it off. Not going to have you troubled, lad, by that.

FENCHURCH. Sod off.

> (*They laugh.*
> WALSH, *groaning, collapses on the bench.*)

WALSH. I'm done. I'm finished. I shall never walk again. Sandy ... Bring us a cup o' tea, old lad.

SANDFORD. You'll have a cup o' bloody nothing. Have a swab at that.

> (*Splashes a cold sponge in* WALSH's *face and round his neck.*
> WALSH *splutters, groans; finally wipes his face and neck.*
> CROSBY *has come in with the remainder of the players.*)

CROSBY. Well done. Well done. Start putting on the pressure in the second half.

JAGGER. Pressure?

FENCHURCH. Pressure ...

JAGGER. That *was* the bloody pressure. Anything from now on is strictly left-overs, Danny lad ... I'm knackered. Look at that. Use hammers on that bloody pitch out theer ...

MACKENDRICK. Well done, then, lads. Well done.

FIELDING.You watching in here, then, Mr Mackendrick, are you?

MACKENDRICK. Out there, old lad. I wouldn't miss it.

CLEGG. See that last try ... ?

MACKENDRICK. ... Go down in the bloody book will that.

SANDFORD. Keep moving. Don't sit still.

CROSBY. That's right. Keep moving ... Walshy. Get up off your arse.

> (WALSH *takes no notice, drinks from bottle.*)

Bryan? How's your ankle?

ATKINSON. All right. I think. It'll be all right.

FIELDING. Just look at that. Can't move me bloody finger.

CROSBY. Keep away from that bloody fire ... Sandy: keep 'em moving round, old lad.

(LUKE *and* SANDFORD *are examining individual players.* MOORE *and* SPENCER *are helping out with laces, tightening boots, handing round the bottles.*)

Any new jerseys? Any new shorts?

(*A couple of players call: 'No ... No thanks.'*)

COPLEY. Over here, lads ... I'll have one ...

CROSBY. Trevor? How's your hands?

TREVOR. All right. (*Holds them up, freezing.*)

CROSBY. Keep moving, lad. Keep shifting.

TREVOR. Be all right. (*He is quite cold: hands and arms folded, then rubbing himself, trying to get warm.*)

CROSBY. Barry?

COPLEY. No. No. All right.

STRINGER. Bloody cold out theer. I read it i' the paper. Seven degrees of frost last night.

SANDFORD. Bloody well move faster, lad.

STRINGER. I am moving faster. It bloody catches up with you.

KENDAL. Ears, look. Can't bloody feel 'em.

JAGGER. Still on, then, Kenny, are they?

KENDAL. Aye. Think so. Better have a look. (*Crosses to mirror.*)

(*They're gradually getting over their first shock of entering the warmer room: sucking sponges, rinsing their mouths from the bottle, rubbing on more grease, adjusting boot-fastenings and socks. Those on the move move quite slowly, tired, panting.*)

FENCHURCH. What's the bloody score, then, lads?

FIELDING. Never notices on the bloody wing.

COPLEY. Picking his bloody nose.

51

FIELDING. Talking to the crowd.

MOORE. Seven–seven, Fenny, lad.

CLEGG (*to* MOORE *and* SPENCER). Bloody cold, you lads, out theer.

SPENCER. Freezing.

MOORE. Fro'zen.

WALSH. Mr Crosby, sir.

CROSBY. What's that?

WALSH. Isn't it time we had a substitute out theer. These lads are dying to get on and lake.

CROSBY. They'll get on in *my* bloody time, not yours. Now get up. Come on. Get moving. I've told thee, Walsh, before.

> (PATSY *is sitting down, having his leg 'stretched' by* SAND-FORD: PATSY'*s leg stretched out before him,* SANDFORD *pressing back the toe of his boot.*)

> (*To* PATSY) You all right?

PATSY. Bloody cramp. God ... (*Groans, winces.*)

WALSH. Another bloody fairy ...

CLEGG. Go on. Give him summat, Sandy ...

WALSH. Here. Let's have a bloody hold.

PATSY. S'all right. S'all right. S'all right. (*Springs up, flexes leg.*)

WALSH. S'all in the bloody mind, tha knows ... Here. Have a look at my bloody back, then, will you?

> (SANDFORD *lifts his jersey at the back.*)

SANDFORD. Got a cut.

WALSH. How many stitches?

SANDFORD. Twenty or thi'ty. Can't be sure.

WALSH. Go on. Go on. Get shut ...

> (*Players laugh.*)

Fieldy: have a bloody look, old lad.

> (FIELDING *lifts* WALSH'*s shirt and looks; slaps* WALSH'*s back.* WALSH *goes over to the bucket, gets sponge, squeezes it down his back.*)

LUKE (*calling, with liniment, etc.*). Any more for any more?

JAGGER. Any bruises, cuts, concussions, fractures ...

COPLEY. One down here you could have a look at, Lukey.
(*Opens shorts: players laugh.*

THORNTON *has come in from the porch entrance.*)

THORNTON. Well played, lads. Well done ... Morley: bloody fine try was that, young man.

MORLEY. Thank you, sir.

THORNTON (*to* CROSBY). Not often we see a run like that ...

CROSBY. No. That's right.

THORNTON. Good kick, Clifford. Good kick was that.

OWENS. Aye. (*During this period he has been out, through the bath entrance, to wash his face and hands, almost like an office worker set for home. Has come in now, drying face and hands.*)

THORNTON. Trevor: dropped goal: a bloody picture.

TREVOR. Thanks.

THORNTON. How're your hands?

TREVOR. Frozen.

THORNTON. Saw you catch that ball: didn't know you'd got it. (*Laughs.*)

TREVOR. Numb ... (*Laughs: rubs his hands.*)

THORNTON. Kenny.
(KENDAL *nods.*)

WALSH. Sir Frederick: how d'you think I managed, then?

THORNTON. Like a dream, Walshy. Like a dream.

JAGGER. Bloody nightmare, I should think, more likely.
(*The players laugh.*)

CROSBY. He could bloody well do wi' wekening up ... There's half on you asleep out yon ... Fieldy ... Bryan ... *move across. Go with it* ... It's no good waiting till they come ... Bloody hell ... Trevor theer: he's covering all that side ... Colin: *bloody interceptions*: it's no good going in, lad, every time ... they'll be bloody well waiting for it

soon ... three times that *I* saw, Jack here had to take your
man ...

WALSH. Billy?

SPENCER. Aye?

WALSH. Go eavesdrop at their door, old lad.

SPENCER (*laughs*). Aye!

WALSH. Find out all their plans.

(*They laugh.*)

CROSBY. As for bloody Walsh. A boot up the backside
wouldn't go astray. I'll swear at times thy's running
bloody backwards, lad.

WALSH. I am. I bloody am ... Too bloody cold today for
running forr'ad.

(*They laugh.* WALSH *claps his cold hands either side of*
SANDFORD's *face.* SANDFORD, *saying, 'Gerroff,' steps
back.*

CROSBY *goes into private, whispered conversation with
individual players.*)

MACKENDRICK. How're you feeling, Trevor, lad?

TREVOR. All right.

MACKENDRICK. Cut your ear there, lad ... (*Examines it.*) Not
bad ... Sandy? ... Put a spot o' grease on that.

(SANDFORD *comes across.* TREVOR *winces.*)

Take care of the professional men, you know. These lot—
(*gestures round*) bloody ten a penny.

(*Jeers.* MACKENDRICK *takes no notice.*)

Have you ever tried playing i' mittens, then?

TREVOR. No.

MACKENDRICK. Some players do, you know. Particularly in
your position ... In the amateur game, you know ... Still.
No need to tell you that, I'm sure.

TREVOR. Aye ... I'll ... just pop off in theer. Shan't be a
minute.

MACKENDRICK. Aye ... aye! (*Slaps his back.*)

(TREVOR *goes off through bath entrance.*
*Electric bell rings.*)

CROSBY. All right. All right. I'm saying no more. Quick score
at the beginning: be all right ... Cliff. At the fourth tackle,
Cliff, try number five. (*To the rest*) Have you got that?

PLAYERS. Aye.

CROSBY. Be bloody ready ... Patsy?

PATSY. Aye.

CROSBY. Fenny?

FENCHURCH. Aye. All right.

CROSBY. Get *up* there! Bloody well stuck in.

FENCHURCH. Aye.

CROSBY. Bryan ...

ATKINSON. Aye.

CROSBY. Harder. *Harder* ... Kenny?

KENDAL. Aye?

CROSBY. *Bang 'em!* You're not tucking the buggers up in
bed.

KENDAL. Aye.

CROSBY. Let's bloody well see it, then ... I want to *hear* those
sods go down ... I want to feel that bloody stand start
shaking ... Johnny: have you got that, lad?

CLEGG. Aye.

CROSBY. Good possession ... If their hooker causes any
trouble let *Walshy* bang his head.

WALSH. I already have done, lad. Don't worry.

(*They laugh.*)

CROSBY. Cliff? Ought you want to add?

OWENS. No. No. Mark your man. Don't wait for somebody
else to take him.

(*Roar of the crowd off.*
*They look to* THORNTON, *who's been going round to
individual players, nodding formally, advising, giving praise.*
TREVOR *comes back in.*)

THORNTON. Good luck, lads. Keep at it. Don't let the pressure drop. Remember: it's thy advantage second half. Away from home, for them: it always tells.

CROSBY. Aye ...

THORNTON. Good luck.

PLAYERS (*uninterested*). Aye ... thanks ...

THORNTON. Go up and shake them lads out o' the bloody boardroom, Mac ... They'll watch the match from up theer if they get half a chance ...

MACKENDRICK. Aye ... Good luck, lads. Don't let up.

PLAYERS. No ... Aye ...

MACKENDRICK. See you after. Keep it up. Well done ... (*On his way out*) Well done ... Well done, Trev. (*Slaps* TREVOR's *back as he goes.*)

(THORNTON *smiles round, nods at* CROSBY, *then follows* MACKENDRICK *out.*)

CROSBY. Watch Tallon near your line.

PLAYERS (*moving off*). Aye ... aye.

OWENS. All right, then, lads. We're off ...

CROSBY. Barry ...

COPLEY (*on move out, hands clenched*). Aye.

CROSBY. Are you listening ...

COPLEY. Aye. Aye. Don't worry.

CROSBY. Right, then ... Fieldy: how's thy eye?

FIELDING. All right.

CROSBY. It's bloody well opened. (*To* LUKE) Look.

FIELDING. Aye. Aye. It'll be all right. (*Dismisses it, goes.*)

CROSBY. Remember ... Fenny ... Patsy ...

PLAYERS (*filing out*). Aye ... aye ... All right.

(*They go.* CROSBY *nods to each one at the door, advising, slapping backs.*

LUKE *and* SANDFORD *start collecting the kit to take out.* MOORE *and* SPENCER *still in their track-suits, pick up a bucket and a bag between them, waiting to follow* CROSBY

*out after the players have gone.*
*Roar of the crowd off as the players go out.*
HARRY *has come in to collect the towels, tapes, bottles, etc.,*
*left lying around.*)

LUKE (*packing his bag*). See you out theer, Danny ...
CROSBY. Right ... Frank ... Billy?
SPENCER. Aye.
CROSBY. Right ...
  (*They go.*
  SANDFORD, LUKE *and* HARRY *are left.*)
LUKE. Well, then, Harry ... How's t'a barn?
HARRY. All right.
LUKE. Been warming up in here, then, have you?
HARRY. I bloody haven't.
SANDFORD (*warming hands at fire*). I'm not so sure I wouldn't
  prefer it here meself.
  (*Crowd roars off.*)
  Ay up. Ay up. That's it. We're off. (*He zips up his track-
  suit top, pulls his scarf round his neck.*)
LUKE. Be with you in a sec, old lad.
SANDFORD. All right. (*Goes.*)
  (LUKE *and* HARRY *work in silence for a moment.*)
LUKE. Do you ever back on matches, Harry?
HARRY. What?
LUKE. Bookies.
HARRY. I don't.
LUKE. Nor 'osses?
HARRY. Nowt.
LUKE. What do you do in your spare time, then?
HARRY. I don't have any spare time.
LUKE. What do you do when you're not up here, then?
HARRY. I'm alus up here.
LUKE. Sleep up here, then, do you?
  (*Roar off.* LUKE *raises head, listens: packs his bag.*)

HARRY. I sleep at home.

LUKE. Where's home?

HARRY. Home's in our house. That's where home is.

LUKE. A damn good place to have it, lad.

HARRY. Bloody keep it theer, an' all.

LUKE. Thornton here, then, was he: first half?

HARRY. Aye.

LUKE. Crafty … He'll never put himself out, you know, unduly.

HARRY. And Mackendrick.

LUKE. Where one goes his shadder follows.

HARRY. It's his place … He can do what he likes … He can sit in here the whole afternoon if he bloody likes.

LUKE. I suppose he can.

> (*Roar off.*)

F'un him up here, you know, one night.

HARRY. What's that?

LUKE. Sir Frederick … Came back one night … Left me tackle … Saw a light up in the stand … Saw him sitting theer. Alone. Crouched up. Like that.

HARRY. His stand. Can sit theer when he likes.

LUKE. Ten o'clock at night.

HARRY. Ten o'clock i' the bloody morning. Any time he likes.

> (LUKE *fastens his bag.*)

LUKE. Is it true, then, what they say?

HARRY. What's that?

LUKE. Thy's never watched a match.

HARRY. Never.

LUKE. Why's that?

HARRY. My job's in here. Thy job's out yonder.

LUKE. They ought to set thee on a pair o' bloody rails. (*Goes over to the door.*)

HARRY. Most jobs you get: they're bloody nowt …

> (LUKE *pauses at the door.*)

Don't know what they work for …

LUKE. What?

HARRY. Not any more. Not like it was ...

LUKE. Well, thy works for the bloody club.

HARRY. I work for Sir Frederick, lad: for nob'dy else.

> (LUKE *looks across at him.*)

I mun run the bloody bath. (*He goes.*)

> (LUKE *watches from the door, then looks round for anything he's forgotten. Comes back in, gets scissors. Sound off, from the bath entrance, of running water. He crosses to the door and goes.*
>
> HARRY *comes back a moment later. He gets towels from the basket and lays them out on the bench, by each peg. At one point there's a roar and booing from the crowd, trumpets, rattles. It dies away to a fainter moan.* HARRY *turns on the Tannoy.*)

TANNOY (*accompanied by roaring of the crowd*). ' ... Copley ... Clegg ... Morley ... Fenchurch! ... inside ... passes ... Jagger ... Stringer ... Tackled. Fourth tackle. Scrum down. Walsh ... Fielding ... Walsh having words with his opposite number! Getting down. The scrum is just inside United's half ... almost ten yards in from the opposite touch ... put in ... some rough play inside that scrum ... Referee Tallon's blown up ... free kick ... no ... scrum down ... not satisfied with the tunnel ... ball in ... Walsh's head is up ... (*Laughter.*) There's some rough business inside that scrum ... my goodness! ... Ball comes out ... Morley ... Copley ... Owens ... Owens to Trevor ... *Trevor is going to drop a goal* ... too late ... He's left it far too late ... They've tried that once before ... Kendal ... '

> (HARRY *switches the Tannoy off.*
> *Great roar outside.*
> HARRY *has crossed to the fire; more coal; pokes it. Goes off to the bath entrance.*)

*A moment later the door from the porch opens:* SANDFORD *comes in.)*

SANDFORD (*calling*). Luke? ... Luke?

HARRY (*re-emerging*). He's just gone ...

SANDFORD. Oh, Christ ...

HARRY. Anything up?

SANDFORD. Gone through the bloody tunnel ... Missed him.
     (*Roar increasing off.* SANDFORD *hurries out.* HARRY *stands in the centre of the room waiting. Baying of the crowd. A few moments later, voices off: 'Hold the bloody door.' 'This side.' 'This side.' 'Take his shoulder.' 'I'm all right. I'm all right. Don't worry.'*
     *The door opens:* KENDAL *comes in, supported by* CROSBY *and* MOORE.)

KENDAL. It's all right ... It's bloody nowt ... Where is it? Where's he put it?

CROSBY. Get him down ... no, over here. Over here. On this. (*They take him to the massage table.*)

KENDAL. Now, don't worry. Don't worry ... Don't worry. I'll be all right ...

MOORE. S'all right, Kenny, lad. All right.

CROSBY. Doesn't know where he is ... Now, come on. Lie down, Kenny, lad. Lie down.

KENDAL. S'all right. S'all right.

CROSBY. Where's bloody Lukey ... Frank: get us a bloody sponge. Harry: o'd him down.
     (CROSBY *tries to hold* KENDAL *down: having been laid on the table, he keeps trying to sit up.*
     HARRY *comes over to the table. He watches, but doesn't help.*)

HARRY (*to* MOORE). Over theer ... that bucket.
     (MOORE *goes off to the bath entrance.*)

CROSBY. Come on, Kenny. Come on ... Lie down, lad.

KENDAL. S'all right ... S'all right ... I'll go back on.

CROSBY. You'll go nowhere, lad ... Come on ... Come on,

then, Kenny, lad. Lie still. I want to bloody look ...
Come on ...

(*The door opens:* SANDFORD *comes in, followed by* LUKE
*with his bag.*)

LUKE. How is he? ... Don't move him ... Let's have a look.

CROSBY. Where's thy been? ... On thy bloody holidays,
hast tha?

LUKE. Let's have a look ... I was coming up ...

CROSBY. Nose ...

(*Steps back,* SANDFORD *takes hold.*

CROSBY *gets a towel, wipes his hands.*)

KENDAL. Nose ... It's me nose, Lukey ...

LUKE. Lie still, lad, now. Lie still.

KENDAL. I can't bloody see, Lukey ...

LUKE. Now just lie still ... That's it ... That's right ...

(MOORE *has brought the sponge.*)

Get some clean water, lad. That's no good ...

SANDFORD. Here ... here ... I'll get it. (*To* MOORE) Come
round here. Get o'd o' this.

(MOORE *takes* SANDFORD's *place.*

SANDFORD *goes off to bath entrance.*

LUKE *has looked at* KENDAL's *wound.* KENDAL's *face is
covered in blood.* LUKE *sponges round his cheeks and mouth,
then stoops down to his bag, gets out cotton-wool.* KENDAL
*is still trying to get up.*)

MOORE. It's all right, Kenny, lad. All right.

KENDAL. Can't see ...

LUKE. Now just keep your eyes closed, lad ... Harry: can you
get a towel?

MOORE. I don't think Ken wa' even looking ... His bloody
head came down ... bloody boot came up ...

(HARRY *has passed over a towel.* MOORE *takes it.*)

LUKE. Shove it underneath his head ... Kenny? Keep your
head still, lad.

(SANDFORD *has brought in a bowl of water.*

LUKE *wipes away the blood with cotton-wool, examines the* *damage.* SANDFORD *pours a drop of disinfectant from the* *bottle into the bowl of water.* LUKE *dips in the cotton-wool,* *wipes* KENDAL's *nose.*

CROSBY, *not really interested, having wiped the blood from* *his hands and his track-suit, looks on impatiently over* LUKE's *back.*)

KENDAL. A bit o' plaster: I'll go back on.

LUKE. Nay, lad. The game's over for you today.

KENDAL. I'll be all right ... I'll get back on ...

CROSBY. He's off, then, is he?

LUKE. Aye ...

SANDFORD. Aye ... (*Gestures up.*) I'll take him up.

CROSBY. Right ... Frank. Come on. Not have you hanging about down here.

SANDFORD. Who you sending on?

CROSBY (*looks round; to* FRANK). Do you think you can manage, then, out theer?

MOORE. Aye!

CROSBY. Come on, then. Let's have you up.

(MOORE, *quickly, jubilantly, strips off his track-suit.*)

Lukey ...

LUKE. Aye.

CROSBY. As soon as you've done. Let's have you up ... Kenny: do you hear that, lad?

KENDAL (*half-rising*). Aye ...

CROSBY. Well done, lad ... Just do as Lukey says ...

KENDAL. Aye ...

CROSBY (*to* MOORE). Come on. Come on. Not ready yet ...

(*Has gone to the door.* MOORE *scrambles out of the suit.* CROSBY *goes.* MOORE, *flexing his legs, pulling down his* *jersey, etc., hesitates.*

*He goes.*)

LUKE. Theer, then, Kenny ...

    (LUKE *has finished washing the wound and has dressed it with a plaster. He now helps* KENDAL *up with* SANDFORD's *assistance*.)

If there's ought you want, just give a shout.

KENDAL. There's me electric tool-kit, Luke ...

LUKE. I've got it here, old lad ... Thy'll be all right ...

KENDAL. Fifteen quid that cost ... just o'er ...

SANDFORD. Here, then. Come on ... Let's have you in the bath. Come on. Come on, now ... It wouldn't do you much good if you dropped it in ...

    (KENDAL *has got up from the table.*

    SANDFORD *helps him over to the bath entrance.*

    LUKE *finishes packing his bag.*

    *The porch door opens:* MACKENDRICK *comes in.*)

MACKENDRICK. How is he?

LUKE. He'll be all right.

MACKENDRICK. Too bloody old, you know. If I've said it once, I've said it ...

LUKE. Aye.

MACKENDRICK (*calls through*). How're you feeling, Kenny, lad.

KENDAL (*off*). All right.

MACKENDRICK. All right, Sandy?

SANDFORD (*off*). Aye. I'll have him in the bath.

MACKENDRICK. Taking him up ... ? (*Gestures up.*)

SANDFORD (*off*). Aye.

MACKENDRICK. I'll see about a car.

SANDFORD (*off*). Shan't be long.

MACKENDRICK (*to* LUKE). I'll go up to the office.

LUKE. Tool-kit. (*Shows him.*)

    (MACKENDRICK *looks in.*)

    Bloody shelves ...

MACKENDRICK. Poor old Kenny ...

LUKE. Bloody wife.

MACKENDRICK. Like that, then, is it?

LUKE. Been round half the teams i' the bloody league ... one time or another. (*Packs his bag and goes over to the bath entrance.*) I'll get on up, then, Sandy, lad.

SANDFORD (*off*). Aye.

LUKE. Be all right, then, Kenny, lad?

KENDAL (*off*). Aye ...

(LUKE *collects his bag.*)

LUKE. You'll see about a taxi, then?

MACKENDRICK. Aye.

(*Roar off.*
*They lift their heads.*)

LUKE. Another score.

MACKENDRICK (*gestures at bath entrance*). I'll get up and tell Sir Freddy, then.

(MACKENDRICK *goes out by the office entrance,* LUKE *by the porch.*

HARRY *is left alone. He's cleared up the bits of cotton-wool and lint; he collects the used towels.*

SANDFORD *brings in* KENDAL'*s used kit, drops it on the floor. Gets a towel.*)

SANDFORD. Take care of that, then, Harry ...

HARRY. Aye.

SANDFORD. Them his clothes?

HARRY. Aye.

(SANDFORD *gets them down. He goes to the bath entrance with the towel.*)

SANDFORD (*off*). Come on, then, Kenny ... Let's have you out.

(HARRY *retidies the massage table, resetting the head-rest which, for* KENDAL'*s sake, has been lowered.*

*A moment later* KENDAL'*s led in with a towel round him.*)

Can you see ought?

KENDAL. Bloody dots ...

SANDFORD. No, this way, lad, then. Over here.

KENDAL. Is the game over, Sandy ... ?

SANDFORD. Just about. Sit theer. I'll get you dried ...

> (KENDAL *sits on the bench.* SANDFORD *dries his legs and feet, then he dries his head.*
>
> HARRY *looks on.*)

Pass his shirt, then, will you?

> (HARRY *passes* KENDAL's *shirt and vest over.*
> *There's a roaring of the crowd off.*)

KENDAL. Are we winning?

SANDFORD. Come on, then ... Get your head in this.

KENDAL. Can't remember ...

> (SANDFORD *pulls his vest and shirt round his head.* KENDAL *dazedly pushes in his arms.*)

HARRY. What's he done?

SANDFORD. Nose.

HARRY. Bro'k it, has he?

SANDFORD. Aye.

KENDAL. Remember shopping.

SANDFORD. We've got it here, old lad. Don't worry.

KENDAL. Bloody fifteen quid ...

HARRY. F'ust one this year.

SANDFORD. Come on, then, lad ... Let's have you up.

> (SANDFORD *helps* KENDAL *to his feet.*
> HARRY *watches, hands in pockets.*
> KENDAL *leans on* SANDFORD. SANDFORD *pulls on his trousers.*)

HARRY. Three collar-bones we had one week ... Two o' theirs ... the last un ours ... Ankle ... Bloody thigh-bone, once ... Red hair ... He never played again.

SANDFORD (*to* KENDAL). Come on, come on, then, lad ... o'd up.

KENDAL. Steam-boilers, lad ... Bang 'em in ... Seen nothing like it. Row o' rivets ... Christ ... Can hardly see ought ... Sandy?

SANDFORD. Here, old lad. Now just hold tight ... Come on.

Come on, now. Let's have you out of here ... (*To*
HARRY) Will you see if Mr Mackendrick's got that car? ...
(*As* HARRY *goes*) Harry: can you find me coat as well?
　　(HARRY *goes, stiffly, leaving by office entry.*
　　*Roar off, rises to peak, applause, bugles, rattles.*
　　KENDAL *turns towards sound, as if to go.*)
Nay, lad: can't go with nothing on your feet.
　　(*Sits* KENDAL *down, puts on his socks and shoes.*)
KENDAL (*dazed*). Started lakin' here when I wa' fifteen, tha
　　knows ... Intermediates ... Then I went out, on loan,
　　to one of these bloody colliery teams ... bring 'em up at
　　the bloody weekend in bloody buckets ... play a game o'
　　bloody football...booze all Sunday...back down at the coal-
　　face Monday ... Seen nothing like it. Better ring my wife.
SANDFORD. What?
KENDAL. She won't know.
SANDFORD. She's not here today, then?
KENDAL. No ...
SANDFORD. I'll see about it, lad. Don't worry.
KENDAL. If I'm bloody kept in, or ought ...
SANDFORD. Aye. It'll be all right.
KENDAL. The woman next door has got a phone.
SANDFORD. Aye. I'll see about it, lad. All right. (*Gets up.*)
　　Let's have your coat on. Won't bother with your tie.
　　(KENDAL *stands.* SANDFORD *helps him into his raincoat.*)
KENDAL. I wa' going to get a new un ... until I bought this
　　drill ...
SANDFORD. Aye! (*Laughs.*)
KENDAL. Start saving up again ...
SANDFORD. That's right.
　　(HARRY *comes in through the office door. He brings in*
　　SANDFORD's *overcoat.*)
HARRY. There's one outside already.
SANDFORD. Good.

HARRY (*watches* SANDFORD's *efforts*). Alus one or two out theer.

SANDFORD. Yeh.

HARRY. Sat'days.

SANDFORD. Could alus use Sir Frederick's, then.

HARRY. Aye ...

SANDFORD. How're you feeling, lad?

KENDAL. All right.

SANDFORD. Come on, then, lad ... Just fasten this ...

(KENDAL *holds his head up so* SANDFORD *can fasten on the dressing Luke has left. It covers his nose and is fastened with plaster to his cheeks.*)

KENDAL. Is it broke?

SANDFORD. There's a bit of a gash, old lad.

KENDAL. Had it broken once before ...

SANDFORD. Can you manage to the car? (*Collects his coat.*)

KENDAL. Wheer is it, then? (*Turns either way.*)

SANDFORD. Here it is, old lad ... (*Hands him his parcel.*)

KENDAL. Have to get some glasses ... hardly see ...

SANDFORD (*to* HARRY). Looks like bloody Genghis Khan ... Come on, then, Kenny ... Lean on me. (*To* HARRY) Still got me bloody boots on ... I'll get them in the office ... See you, lad.

(HARRY *watches them go.*
*He waits. Then he picks up the used towel, takes it off to dump inside the bath entrance.*
*He comes back, looks round, switches on the Tannoy.*)

TANNOY. (*Crowd roar.*) ' ... to Walsh ... reaches the twenty-five ... goes down ... plays back ... (*Roar.*) ... Comes to Clegg to Atkinson ... Atkinson to the substitute Moore ... Moore in now, crashes his way through ... goes down ... Walsh comes up ... out to Owens ... Owens through ... dummies ... beautiful move ... to Stringer, Stringer out to Patsy ... Patsy out to Trevor, who's come up on the wing ... kicks ... Copley ... Fenchurch ... Fielding ... *Morley* ...

(*Roar.*) Ball bounces into touch ... scrum ... (*Pause, dull roar.*) Growing dark now ... ball goes in, comes out, Tallon blows ... free kick ... scrum infringement ... one or two tired figures there ... can see the steam, now, rising from the backs ... Trevor's running up and down, blowing in his hands ... Kick ... good kick ... (*Crowd roar.*) Finds touch beyond the twenty-five ... (*Crowd roar.*)

(HARRY *sits, listening.*
*Fade: sound and light.*)

# ACT THREE

*The same.*

*Noise: shouting, singing, screeching, cries off. The Tannoy is playing music.*

PATSY, *a towel round his waist, is drying himself with a second towel, standing by his clothes. He does it with the same care with which he prepared himself for the match.*

HARRY *is picking up the mass of discarded shorts, jerseys, jock-straps, and putting them on the basket.*

*A pile of towels stands on the rubbing-down table.*

SPENCER *is half-dressed in trousers and shirt, combing his wet hair in the mirror.*

CROSBY *is going round checking boots, putting pairs together by the massage table to be collected up.*

CROSBY (*to* SPENCER). Up there waiting for you, is she, Billy?

SPENCER. Aye. All being well. (*Combing in mirror.*) Bloody expecting me to play today, an' all.

CROSBY. Ne'er mind. Next week: might be in luck.

SPENCER. Bloody away next week!

CROSBY. Maybe she'll have to bloody travel.

SPENCER. Not the travelling kind, you know.

CROSBY. Can't win 'em all, old lad. Don't worry ... (*Calls*) Come on. Let's have you out o' there ... (*Switches off Tannoy, moves on. To* PATSY) How're you feeling, then, old lad?

PATSY. All right. Bit stiff. (*Winces: eases arm.*)

CROSBY. How's thy shoulder?

PATSY. All right.

69

CROSBY. Bloody lovely try. Worth any amount o' bloody knocks is that.

PATSY. Aye.

CROSBY. Couple more next week ... should be all right.

PATSY. Aye. (*Doesn't respond, drying himself, turns to check his clothes.*)

> (JAGGER *comes bursting in from the bath.*)

JAGGER. Dirty bugger ... dirty sod ... Danny: go bloody stop him. (*Snatches towel, rubs his hair vigorously.*) Walshy — pittling in the bloody bath.

SPENCER (*calling through*). Thy'll have to disinfect that bloody water ... (*Laughing.*)

WALSH (*off*). This *is* disinfectant, lad.

CROSBY. Come on, Walshy: let's have you out ...

> (*Takes a towel and dries* JAGGER's *back.*)

JAGGER. Dirty bugger: dirty sod!

WALSH (*off*). Come on, Jagger. You could do with a bloody wash.

JAGGER. Not in that, you dirty sod ... Set bloody Patsy onto you, if you don't watch out.

> (*Water comes in from the bath.*)

Dirty! Dirty! ...

> (*Dances out of the way: laughter and shouting off.*)

CROSBY. Come on, Trevor. Teach 'em one or two manners, then ... Bloody college-man ... going to go away disgusted with all you bloody working lads.

> (*Another jet of water.* CROSBY *lurches out of the way.*)

Bloody well be in there if you don't watch out.

> (*Jeers, cries.*)

COPLEY (*off*). Too bloody old!

CLEGG (*off*). Come on, Danny. Show us what you've got.

CROSBY. Got summat here that'll bloody well surprise you, lad ...

> (*Laughter, cries.*)

And you!

(*Laughter off.*)

Sithee ... Billy. Go in and quieten 'em down.

SPENCER. Nay ... gotten out in one bloody piece. Not likely.
Send Harry in. He'll shift 'em out.

(HARRY *looks up: they laugh. He doesn't respond.*
*Singing starts off, then all join in from the bath.*
LUKE *comes in.*)

CROSBY. Got through, then, did you?

LUKE. He'll be all right ...

JAGGER. Kenny?

LUKE. Broken nose.

JAGGER. Keeping him in, then, are they?

LUKE. Aye.

JAGGER. Give his missus chance to bloody roam.

LUKE (*goes over to* PATSY). How's it feel, old lad?

PATSY. All right. (*Eases his shoulder, stiffly.*)

LUKE. Come in tomorrow: I'll give you a bloody rub.

PATSY. Right.

LUKE. Need a drop of stuff on theer. (*Goes to his bag.*)

(TREVOR *has come in, wiping himself down with a towel.*)

TREVOR. Just look ... just beginning to get up circulation ...
(*Flexes his fingers.*)

JAGGER. Circulate a bit lower down for me.

(CROSBY *has a towel and now dries* TREVOR's *back.*)

TREVOR. Bloody shaking, still. Just look. (*Holds out his hands,*
*trembling.*)

CROSBY. Don't worry. This time tomorrow ...

(*Flicks towel to* SPENCER, *who finishes rubbing* TREVOR's
*back.*)

SPENCER. What's thy teach, then, Trev?

TREVOR. Mathematics.

SPENCER. Maths ...

TREVOR. One of your subjects, is it?

SPENCER. One ... (*Laughs.*)

LUKE. T'other's bloody lasses, Trev.

SPENCER. Nay, I gi'e time o'er to one or two other things, an' all.

(*They laugh.*)

JAGGER. Here ... Got the two-thirty, Lukey, have you?

LUKE. Somewheer ... (*Tosses the paper over from his pocket.*)

SPENCER (*to* TREVOR). That kind o' mathematics, Trev.

(*Slaps* TREVOR'S *back: finished drying.*)

TREVOR. Shoulda known. (*Turns away to get dressed.*)

JAGGER. Let me see ... (*Examines stop-press.*) One-thirty ... (*To* SPENCER) Quite a bit fastened up in that ... (*Reading*) Two o'clock ... Two-thirty ... No ...

CROSBY. What's that, Jagger, lad?

(JAGGER *tosses paper down. Goes to his clothes.*)

SPENCER. Let's have a look.

JAGGER (*to* LUKE). Don't say a word to bloody Walsh.

LUKE. Shan't say a word. (*Laughs.*) Not a sausage.

(LUKE *has dabbed an orange-staining antiseptic on* PATSY'S *arm; now he crosses to* TREVOR. *As* TREVOR *starts to dress he moves round him, dabbing on antiseptic with cotton-wool.*) Hold still. Hold still.

(CLEGG *comes in, drying.*)

CLEGG. Bit lower down there, Lukey.

LUKE. Aye. (*Laughs.*)

SPENCER (*reading*). Bloody Albatross. Seven to one.

JAGGER. What d'you back, Billy, lad?

SPENCER. Same as you, Jag. Little Nell. (*To* LUKE) Tipped the bloody 'oss himself.

JAGGER. Bloody Walsh ... Never hear the end.

CLEGG. What's that?

(JAGGER, *dry, has started to dress.*

SPENCER *has taken the towel from* CLEGG *and is drying his back.*)

JAGGER. Albatross: come up ... (*Gestures off.*)

CLEGG (*to* SPENCER). What's that?

SPENCER. I'm saying nowt.

> (*Flicks the towel to* CLEGG, *picks up another.*
>
> COPLEY *has come in, followed by* FENCHURCH. SPENCER
> *goes to dry* COPLEY's *back,* CROSBY *to dry* FENCHURCH's.)

COPLEY. Sithee, there ought to be a special bloody bath for those dirty bloody buggers: I'm muckier now than when I bloody well went in.

WALSH (*off, siren-call*). Barry! Barry! *We can't do without you, Barry!*

COPLEY (*calling*). Sod off.

MORLEY (*siren, off*). *Barr...y!*

WALSH (*siren, off*). Barr...y ...

MORLEY (*off*). Barr...y! ... We're *waiting*, Barry!

COPLEY (*calling*). Piss off!

CROSBY. Come on, Fieldy ... Keep those ignorant sods in line.

FIELDING (*off*). I'm in the bloody shower. I'm not in with those mucky bloody sods.

JAGGER. How're you feeling, Fenny, lad?

FENCHURCH. All right ... (*Indicating paper*) Results in theer, then, are they?

CLEGG (*has picked it up to read*). Aye. (*Reads*) 'Latest score: twelve–seven.' Patsy: they didn't get thy try ... Sithee: pricked up his bloody ears at that.

> (*They laugh.* PATSY, *having turned, goes back to dressing.*)

FENCHURCH. Fifteen–seven ...

JAGGER. Fifteen–seven.

FENCHURCH. Put a good word in with Sir Frederick, then.

CROSBY. Good word about bloody what, then, lad?

FENCHURCH. Me and Jagger, Danny boy ... Made old Patsy's bloody try ... In't that right, then, Jagger lad?

PATSY. Made me own bloody try. Ask Jack ...

> (STRINGER *has come in, shaking off water.* CROSBY *goes to him with a towel: dries his back.*)

73

MORLEY (*off*). Any more for any more?
   (*Laughter off.*)
WALSH (*off*). Barry...y! *We're waiting, Barry!*
FENCHURCH. Take no notice. Silly sod.
STRINGER. Where's Cliff, then?
JAGGER. Up in the directors' bath, old lad.
STRINGER. Is that right, then?
CROSBY. Captain's privilege, lad.
STRINGER. Bloody hell ... (*Snatches towel, goes over to the
   bench to dry himself.*)
   (LUKE *is still going round, dabbing on antiseptic.*)
LUKE. Any cuts, bruises: ought that needs fastening up?
JAGGER. I've a couple of things here that need a bit of bloody
   attention, Lukey ...
LUKE. What's that?
   (*Goes over;* JAGGER *shows him.*
   *They all laugh.*
   PATSY *has crossed to the mirror to comb his hair.*)
PATSY. Did you see a young woman waiting for me up there,
   Danny?
   (*Groans and jeers from the players.*)
CLEGG. How do you do it, Patsy? I can never make that out.
FENCHURCH. Nay, his girl-friend's a bloody schoolmistress.
   Isn't that right, then, Patsy?
   (PATSY *doesn't answer: combs his hair, straightens his tie.*)
JAGGER. Schoolmistress?
FENCHURCH. Teaches in Trevor's bloody school ... Isn't that
   right, then, Trev?
   (TREVOR *nods, doesn't look up: gets on with his dressing.*)
JAGGER. What do you talk about, then, Patsy?
   (*They laugh.* PATSY *is crossing to his coat. With some care
   he pulls it on.*)
CLEGG (*having gone to him*). The moon in *June* ... Is coming out
   quite *soon*!

74

WALSH (*off*). Barr...y! *Where are you, Barr...y!*

COPLEY. Piss off, you ignorant sod.

MORLEY (*off*). Barr...y! *We're waiting, Barr...y!*
(*Laughter off.*)

LUKE. Sithee ... Can you sign these autograph books: there's half a dozen lads outside ... Clean forgot. (*Takes them from his pocket, puts them on the table.*)

JAGGER. By God: just look at that!
(PATSY *has already crossed to the table.*)
Pen out in a bloody flash ...
(PATSY *takes out a pen clipped to his top pocket. Writes.* JAGGER *stoops over his shoulder to watch.*)
He can write, an' all ... 'Patrick Walter Turner.' Beautiful. Bloody beautiful is that.

PATSY. Piss off.

JAGGER. Here, now. Bloody language, Trev! ... Hears that, she'll never speak again.

FENCHURCH. Put you down in her bloody book ...

JAGGER. Black mark.

FENCHURCH. A thousand lines ...

JAGGER. 'I must not bloody swear, you cunt.'
(*They laugh.*
FIELDING *comes in, picks up a towel.* SPENCER *goes over to dry his back.*)

FIELDING. They're going to be in theer a bloody fo'tnight ... Harry — go in and pull that bloody plug.

HARRY. Aye. (*Doesn't look up.*)
(*Burst of laughter. Shouts off: 'Give over! Give over! You rotten bloody sod!'*)

STRINGER. They could do with putting in separate bloody showers in theer.

CROSBY. What's that, Jack?

STRINGER. Separate showers. It's not hygienic, getting bathed together.

CLEGG. It's not. He's right. That's quite correct.

FENCHURCH. Put a bit o' colour in your cheeks, old lad.

STRINGER. I've got all the colour theer I need.

JAGGER. Played a grand game today, though, Jack. (*Winks at the others.*)

STRINGER. Aye. (*Mollified.*)

JAGGER. Marvellous. Bloody fine example, that.

STRINGER. Aye. Well ... I did my best.

JAGGER. Them bloody forwards: see them clear a way.

(*They laugh.* STRINGER *dries his hair, rubbing fiercely.*
ATKINSON *comes in from the bath, limping.*
CROSBY *gets a towel, dries his back.*)

LUKE. Let's have you on here, Bryan. Let's have a look.

(LUKE *waits by the table while* ATKINSON *gets dry.*)

MORLEY (*off*). Barry! *Where are you, Barry!*

WALSH (*off*). Barry! *We're waiting, Barry ...*

(COPLEY *looks round: sees one of the buckets: takes it to the bath entrance: flings the cold water in.*
*Cries and shouts off.*
*The players laugh.*)

CROSBY. Go on. Here ... Here's a bloody 'nother.

(COPLEY *takes it, flings the water in.*
*Cries, shouts off.*
*The players laugh, looking over at the bath entrance.*
ATKINSON *is dry now and, with a towel round him, he lies down on the massage table.* LUKE *examines his leg.*
PATSY, *having got on his coat, has returned to the mirror. Final adjustments: collar, tie, hair ...*
STRINGER *continues getting dressed.* TREVOR *joins* PATSY *at the mirror.*
FENCHURCH, JAGGER *and* CLEGG *are almost dressed,* FIELDING *just beginning.*)

JAGGER. Go on, Barry! Ought else you've bloody got!

(COPLEY *looks round, sees nothing.*)

CROSBY. Here ... Come on ... Turn on that bloody hose.
(*He picks up the end of the hose by the bath entrance, turns the tap. They spray the water into the bath entrance.*
*Cries and shouts from the bath.*
*The players call out: 'More! More! Go on! All over!'*
*Cries and shouts off. A moment later* MOORE *and* MORLEY *come running in, shaking off water, the players scattering.*)
MOORE. Give over! Give over! Ger off!
(*They grab towels, start rubbing down.*)
WALSH (*off*). More! More! Lovely! Lovely! ... That's it, now, lads ... No. No. Right ... Lovely. Lovely ... Bit lower, Barry ... Lovely! Grand!
(*The players laugh.*)
CROSBY (*to* COPLEY). All right ...
LUKE. That's enough ...
CROSBY. Nowt'll get through that bloody skin, I can tell you. (*Calls through*) We're putting the lights out in ten minutes, lad ... You can stay there all night if tha bloody wants.
(COPLEY *turns off the tap.*
*The players go back to getting dressed.*)
STRINGER. All over me bloody clothes. Just look.
FIELDING. Here ... here, old lad. I'll mop it up ... Grand game today, then, Jack.
STRINGER. Aye ... All right.
(CROSBY *dries* MOORE's *back.* SPENCER *dries* MORLEY's.)
CROSBY. What's it feel like, Frank?
MOORE. Grand ... Just got started.
FIELDING. Knows how to bloody lake, does Frank ... ten minutes ...
MOORE. Nearer thi'ty.
FIELDING. Just time to get his jersey mucky ...
CROSBY. He'll bloody show you lads next week ...
FIELDING. Can't bloody wait to see, old lad.

WALSH (*off*). Barry ... *I'm waiting*, Barry!
    (*The players laugh.*)
COPLEY. Well, I'm bloody well not waiting here for thee!
    (*They laugh.*
    *The door from the office has opened.*
    THORNTON, *followed by* MACKENDRICK, *comes in.*)
THORNTON. Well done, lads ... Bloody champion ... well
    done ... They'll not come here again in a bloody hurry ...
    not feel half so bloody pleased ... How's thy feeling,
    Patsy, lad?
PATSY. All right, sir.
THORNTON. Lovely try ... Bloody text-book, lad ... Hope
    they got that down on bloody film ... Frank? How's it
    feel, young man?
MOORE. Pretty good. All right.
CROSBY. Just got started ...
FIELDING. Just got into his stride, Sir Frederick.
THORNTON. Another ten minutes ... he'd have had a bloody try.
    (*They laugh.*)
   Set 'em a bloody fine example, lad, don't worry. Well
   played there, lad. Well done.
MACKENDRICK. Well done, lad.
THORNTON. How's your leg, then, Bryan?
ATKINSON. Be all right.
    (ATKINSON *is still on the table.* LUKE *is massaging the leg
    with oil.*)
THORNTON. Nasty bloody knock was that.
ATKINSON. Went one way ... Me leg went t'other.
THORNTON (*to* TREVOR). How's your hands now, then, lad?
TREVOR. All right. Fine, thanks. (*Has pulled on his club blazer.*
    *Looks up from dusting it down.*)
THORNTON (*to* FIELDING). I hope you're going to get your
    eye seen to there, old lad.
FIELDING. Aye.

THORNTON. Bad news about old Kenny.

PLAYERS. Aye ...

WALSH (*off*). Barr...y ... I am *waiting*, Barry!

THORNTON. Who's that, then? Bloody Walsh?

CROSBY. Aye.

THORNTON (*going to the bath entrance*). And who's thy waiting for, then, Walshy?

    (*Pause.*)

WALSH (*off*). Oh, good evening, Sir Frederick ...

THORNTON. I'll give you Sir bloody Frederick ... I'll be inside that bath in a bloody minute.

WALSH (*off*). Any time, Sir Frederick, any time is good enough for me.

    (*The players laugh.*

    MACKENDRICK *has moved off amongst the players, going first to* PATSY, *then to* TREVOR, *slapping backs: 'Well done. Good match.'*

    THORNTON *turns back to the players.*)

THORNTON. I think we ought to charge Walsh bloody rent: spends more time here than he does at home.

CROSBY. Thy had five quid off him here last week: swearing to the referee.

MACKENDRICK. That's right. We did!

    (*They laugh.*)

THORNTON. No luck this week, then, I fancy?

CROSBY. Shouldn't think so. Tallon's not above bloody answering back.

THORNTON. Shifty bugger is old Walshy ... Grand try in the first half, Mic. Good game.

MORLEY. Thanks.

    (MORLEY, *his back dried by* SPENCER, *is now getting dressed.*)

THORNTON. Bloody well stuck to you in the second half, I noticed.

MORLEY. Aye ... Hardly room to move about.

THORNTON. Was Kenny's an accident, then ... Or someb'dy catch him?

MORLEY. A bit slow, I think, today.

ATKINSON. Too cold ...

MORLEY. It went right through you.

THORNTON. There's a bloody frost out theer already ... Shouldn't be surprised if it snows tonight ... Jagger: grand game, lad. Well done.

JAGGER. Thanks, Sir Frederick.

THORNTON. Shook their centre a time or two, I saw.

JAGGER. Always goes off the bloody left foot.

THORNTON. So I noticed ... (*To* STRINGER) Well done there, Jack. Well played.

STRINGER. Thanks, Sir Frederick.

THORNTON. One of your best games for a long time, lad ... Not that the others haven't been so bad. (*Laughs.*) Liked your tackling. Stick to it ... Low, low!

STRINGER. Aye! That's right!

THORNTON. Any knocks, bruises?

STRINGER. No. No. Be all right.

THORNTON. Come up tomorrow if you're feeling stiff. Lukey here'll be doing his stuff.

LUKE. Aye ... That's right.

(*He slaps* ATKINSON *who gets up and starts to dress.*)

Gi'e us a couple o' hours i' bed ... mek it ten o'clock, old lad.

(*After wiping his hands* LUKE *starts to check his bottles, cotton-wool, etc., packing them in his bag.*)

THORNTON. Bloody gossip shop is this on a Sunday morning ... Isn't that right, then, Mac?

MACKENDRICK. Aye. It is.

PATSY. I'll ... er ... get off, then, Sir Frederick ... See you next week, then, all being well.

THORNTON. Your young lady waiting, is she?

PATSY. Aye ... I think so.

THORNTON. Grand game. Well done.

PATSY. Thanks, Sir Frederick ... See you next week, Mr Mackendrick.

MACKENDRICK. Aye. Aye. Well done, young man.

PATSY. Bye, lads!

PLAYERS (*without much interest*). Aye ... bye ... cheerio.

MORLEY. Gi'e her a big kiss, then, Patsy, lad.
   (*Chorus of laughter.*)

JAGGER. Gi'e her one for me, an' all.

FENCHURCH. And me.

COPLEY. And me.

FIELDING. And me.

ATKINSON. And me.

CLEGG. And me.

MOORE. And me.

SPENCER. And me, an' all.
   (*They laugh.*
   PATSY *goes: leaves through the porch entrance.*)

MACKENDRICK. Bloody good example there is Pat ... Saves his bloody money ... Not like some.

CLEGG. Saves it for bloody what, though, Mac?

MACKENDRICK. He's got some bloody brains has Pat ... puts it i' the bank, for one ...

FIELDING. Big-headed sod.

CROSBY. What's that?

LUKE. He's got some good qualities has Pat.

FIELDING. I don't know where he keeps them, then.
   (*They laugh.*)

THORNTON (*to* MACKENDRICK). Nay, don't look at me, old lad. (*Laughs. Has gone over to the fire to warm his hands.*)

JAGGER (*calling*). Sing us a song, then, Jack, old love.

STRINGER. Sing a bloody song thysen.

(*They laugh.*

OWENS *has come in from the office, dressed in a smart suit: a neat, cheerful, professional man.*)

OWENS. Look at this. Bloody opening-time. Not even dressed.

MORLEY. Where's thy been, then, Cliff?

JAGGER. Up in Sir Frederick's private shower-room, have you?

OWENS. I thought it might be crowded, lads, today. What with that and the bloody cold ... (*Winks, crosses to the massage table. Loudly*) Got a bit o' plaster, have you, Lukey?

PLAYERS. Give over! Give over! Get off!

OWENS. Got a little cut here ...

PLAYERS. Give over! Give over! Get off!

(OWENS, *winking, goes over to the fire to warm his hands.*)

JAGGER. Give him a bloody kiss, Sir Frederick ... that's all he bloody wants.

(*They laugh.*

WALSH *appears at the bath entrance, a towel around his middle.*

*He stands in the bath entrance, nodding, looking in.*)

WALSH. I thought I could hear him ... (*To* OWENS) Come to see the workers, have you? How long're you going to give us, lad?

OWENS. I'll give thee all the time thy wants, old love.

(*The others laugh.*)

WALSH (*gestures back*). I've been waiting for you, Barry ...

(*The others laugh.*)

FENCHURCH. What's thy want him for, then, Walsh?

CROSBY. What's he after, Barry? What's he want?

WALSH. He knows what I've been waiting for.

(*They laugh.*)

LUKE. We're bloody well closing shop in a couple o' minutes,

Walsh. You want to hurry up. You'll be turned out without thy bloody clothes.

ATKINSON. T'only bloody bath he gets is here.

(*They laugh.* WALSH *still stands there, gazing in, confronted.*)

COPLEY. Come on, then, Walshy. Show us what you've got.

WALSH. I'll show thee bloody nowt, old lad. (*Moves over towards his clothes.*) Keeping me bloody waiting ... sat in theer.

(*They laugh.*)

I was *waiting* for you, Barry ...

(*They laugh.*)

CLEGG. Come on, then, Walshy, lad ...

FENCHURCH. Gi'e us a bloody shock.

MORLEY. Mr Mackendrick, here: he's been hanging on for hours.

(*They laugh.*)

MACKENDRICK. Nay, don't bring me into it, old lad. I've seen all of Walshy that I bloody want.

(WALSH, *with great circumspection, the towel still around him, has started to put on his clothes: vest and shirt.*)

WALSH. Tell my bloody wife about you, Jagger ... Dirty bloody sod ...

CROSBY (*to all of them*). Come on, come on, then. Let's have you out ...

HARRY (*entering*). Have you all finished, then, in theer?

(*Most of the players now are dressed; one or two have started to smoke.* OWENS *and* THORNTON *stand with their backs to the fire, looking on.*

HARRY *has collected up the jerseys, stockings, shorts and towels. He's worked anonymously, overlooked, almost as if, for the players, he wasn't there. Having taken out some of the boots, he comes back in.*)

WALSH. What?

HARRY. Have you finished with that bath?

WALSH. What do you want me to bloody do? Sup the bloody stuff, old lad?

(*They laugh.*)

HARRY. I'll go and empty it, then.

FENCHURCH. Mind how you touch that water, lad.

FIELDING. Bloody poisonous, is that.

(HARRY, *without any response, goes to the hose, takes it in to the bath, reappears, turns the tap, goes off to the bath.*

TALLON *has put his head in from the office entrance. He's dressed in an overcoat and scarf, and carries a small hold-all.*)

TALLON. Just say goodnight, then, lads.

PLAYERS. Aye ... aye ... Goodnight ... Goodnight ...

TALLON. A good game, lads.

CROSBY. Aye.

TALLON. Both sides played very well. And in very difficult conditions, too.

CROSBY. Aye. Aye. That's right.

TALLON. Sorry about Kendal ... I hear they've taken him off.

LUKE. Aye ... He'll be all right.

TALLON. Keeping him in, then, are they?

MACKENDRICK. Aye. That's right.

TALLON. Say goodnight, then, Mr Mackendrick ... See you soon.

(*Crosses, shakes hands with* MACKENDRICK.)

MACKENDRICK. I don't think you've met Sir Frederick.

TALLON. No. No. I haven't.

THORNTON. Admired your refereeing very much.

TALLON. Thank you. Thank you very much, sir.

THORNTON. See you up here again, then, soon, I hope.

TALLON. Aye. Aye. Our job, though, you never know.

THORNTON. If you bring the same result with you, you can come up every bloody week, tha knows.

(*They laugh.*)

Going upstairs, then, are you? (*Mimes drink.*)

TALLON. No. No. I've to catch me train. Otherwise I would. This weather. You can never chance your luck ... Well, goodbye. It's been a pleasure.

(*Nods to* OWENS, *ducks his head to the others, goes.*)

WALSH. Anybody heard the bloody two-thirty?

JAGGER. No.

FENCHURCH. No.

SPENCER. No.

LUKE. No.

FIELDING. No.

MOORE. No.

WALSH (*back to them, getting dressed*). By God, sunk me bloody week's wages theer ... You haven't got a paper, Mac?

MACKENDRICK. No. No. Haven't had a chance.

COPLEY. Let's see. Now here's one ... What wa're it, now?

WALSH (*dressing*). Two-thirty.

COPLEY (*reading*). 'One o'clock ... one-thirty ... two o'clock ... two-fifteen ... '

WALSH. Come on, come on, come on ...

(JAGGER *points it out.*)

COPLEY. Two-thirty! ... Let's see now. What d'thy bet?

WALSH. Just tell us the bloody winner. Come on. Come on.

COPLEY. What's this, now? ... Can't see without me glasses ... Little ... what is it?

WALSH. Oh, God.

COPLEY. Nell.

WALSH. Hell fire ... Can't bloody well go home tonight.

COPLEY (*still reading*). Worth having something on, was that.

WALSH. Tell bloody Jagger: don't tell me.

JAGGER. And Fenny (*winking*).

WALSH. And Fenny ... Here. Let's have a look.

(*They wait, watching, suppressing their laughter as* WALSH, *eyes screwed up, short-sighted, reads.*)

Here! ... Here! ... What's this ... (*Eyes screwed, still reads.*)
(*They burst out laughing.*)

Just look at that. Bloody Albatross! *Seven to one!*
(*Shows it to* ATKINSON *to be confirmed.*)

ATKINSON. That's right.

WALSH. I've won, I've won.
(*Embraces* STRINGER, *who's standing near him, fastening his coat.*)

STRINGER. Go on. Go on. Ger off !
(*The players laugh.*)

WALSH. By God. That's made my bloody day, has that.

MACKENDRICK. More interested in that than he is in bloody football.

WALSH. I am. I am, old lad ... More bloody brass in this for a bloody start. (*Laughs, finishes his dressing.*) By God, then: see old Barry now ... Wish thy'd washed my bloody back, then, don't you?

COPLEY. I think I bloody do. That's right.
(*They laugh.*)

FIELDING. Well, then, lads. I'm off ...

PLAYERS. See you, Fieldy ... Bye.

LUKE. Watch that bloody eye.

FIELDING. Aye. Aye. It'll be all right.

THORNTON. Bye, Fieldy. Well done, lad.

FIELDING. Aye ... (*Goes.*)

JAGGER. Fenny ... Ar' t'a barn, then? ... Trev?

FENCHURCH (*packing his bag*). Aye ...

TREVOR. Aye.

WALSH. Lukey ... where's my bloody cigar, old lad!
(*They laugh.* LUKE *gets out the cigar.*
JAGGER *and* TREVOR *have gone to the door. They're joined by* FENCHURCH *carrying his bag.*)

JAGGER. See you, lads, then.

ALL. Aye.

TREVOR. Bye.

ALL. Bye ... See you.

MACKENDRICK. Well done, Trevor, lad.

TREVOR. Aye ...

> (*They go.*
> WALSH *is lighting up.*)

THORNTON (*going*). Mind you don't choke on that, then, Walshy.

WALSH. Don't bloody worry ... From now on ... Trouble free! (*Blows out a cloud of smoke for his amusement.*)

THORNTON. Bye, lads ... Clifford?

OWENS. Aye. Shan't be a minute.

THORNTON Time for a snifter, lads, tha knows ... (*Gestures up.*)

ALL. Aye ...

COPLEY. Bye, Sir Frederick ...

> (THORNTON *goes through the office entrance.* MACKEN-
> DRICK, *nodding, follows.*
> CROSBY, *picking up a couple of remaining boots, goes off through the bath entrance.*)

STRINGER. Well, I've got everything, I think. I'm off.

COPLEY. Enjoyed yourself today, then, Jack?

STRINGER. Aye. All right.

CLEGG. They tell me your mother was here this afternoon, then, Jack.

STRINGER. As likely.

COPLEY. T'only bloody fan he's got.

STRINGER. I've got one or two more, an' all.

> (*They laugh.*)

ATKINSON. Give you a lift into town, Jack, if you like.

STRINGER. No ... no ... I like to walk. (*He goes.*)

> (*They laugh.*)

WALSH. Here ... Here you are, then, Cliff.

> (WALSH, *having finished dressing, adjusted his buttonhole*

*and combed his hair in the mirror, gets out another cigar.*
*The others watch in amazement.*)

OWENS. Thanks, Walshy ... Thanks very much ... Won't
smoke it now. (*Smells it appreciatively.*)

WALSH. Save it.

OWENS. Appreciate it later.

WALSH. Not like these ignorant bloody sods ...

COPLEY. Well, bloody hell ...

WALSH. Come today, tha knows ... All gone tomorrer.

CLEGG. Bloody hell.

COPLEY. The stingy bugger ...

> (WALSH *laughs: a last look round: coat.*
> CROSBY *comes back in through bath entrance.*)

CROSBY. Come on. Come on. Let's have you out. (*Claps his
hands.*)

CLEGG. A bloody fistful ...

WALSH. Just one. Just one. (*Puffs at his own.*) Just the odd one,
old son.

COPLEY. Greasing round the bloody captain, Danny.

WALSH. Keep in wi' me bloody captain. Never know when
you might need a bloody favour. Isn't that right, then,
Cliff?

OWENS. That's right.

> (*They laugh, going.*)

ATKINSON. Well, then, Walshy ... (*Gestures up.*) Gonna buy
us one?

WALSH. I might ...

> (*They've moved over to the office door, except for* OWENS,
> CROSBY *and* LUKE.
>
> MOORE *stands to one side.*)

Barry here, o' course, will have to do without ... (*To*
CROSBY) Never came when I bloody called ... As for the
rest ... I might stand a round ... Might afford it ... And
one for thee, old lad. All right?

SPENCER. All right.

WALSH (*looking back*). What was Jagger's horse, now?

LUKE. Little Nell.

WALSH. Little Nell! (*He laughs.*)

CLEGG. Are you coming, Frank?

MOORE. Aye. Aye. I will.

WALSH (*to* MOORE). Thy's kept bloody quiet, old lad ...

MOORE. Aye ...

WALSH. Don't let these bloody lads upset you.

MOORE. No. No. (*Laughs.*)

WALSH (*puts his arm round* MOORE's *shoulder, going*). Sithee,
    Barry ... first flush o' bloody success is that.

COPLEY (*leaving*). Mic?

MORLEY. Aye. Just about.

> (*They go, laughing. Burst of laughter and shouts outside.
> Silence.* LUKE *has packed his bag; he zips it up.* CROSBY *is
> picking up the rest of the equipment: odd socks, shirts.
> OWENS gets out a cigarette; offers one to CROSBY who takes
> one, then offers one to LUKE who shakes his head.
> There's a sound of HARRY singing off: hymn.
> OWENS flicks a lighter. Lights CROSBY's cigarette, then
> his own.*)

CROSBY. Not two bloody thoughts to rub together ...
    (*Gestures off.*) Walshy.

OWENS. No. (*Laughs.*)

CROSBY. Years ago ... ran into a bloody post ... out yonder
    ... split the head of any other man ... Gets up: looks
    round: says, 'By God', then ... 'Have they teken him
    off?'

> (*They laugh.* LUKE *swings down his bag.*)

LUKE. I'm off.

CROSBY. See you, Lukey.

LUKE. Cliff ...

OWENS. Thanks, Lukey.

LUKE (*calls*). Bye, Harry …
    (*They wait. Hymn continues.*)
CROSBY. Wandered off … (*Taps his head: indicates Harry off.*)
LUKE. Aye … See you, lads. (*Collects autograph books.*)
OWENS. Bye, Lukey.
    (LUKE *goes with his bag through the porch entrance.*
    CROSBY *picks up the last pieces. Hymn finishes.*)
CROSBY. How're you feeling?
OWENS. Stiff.
CROSBY. Bloody past it, lad, tha knows.
OWENS. Aye. One more season, I think: I'm finished.
    (CROSBY *laughs.*)
  Been here, tha knows, a bit too long.
CROSBY. Nay, there's nob'dy else, old lad …
OWENS. Aye … (*Laughs.*)
CROSBY. Need thee a bit longer to keep these lads in line.
OWENS. Aye. (*Laughs.*)
CROSBY. Did well today.
OWENS. They did. That's right.
CROSBY. Bloody leadership, tha see, that counts.
OWENS (*laughs*). Aye …
CROSBY (*calls through to bath*). Have you finished, then, in theer …
    (*No answer.*)
  (*To* OWENS) Ger up yonder …
OWENS. Have a snifter …
CROSBY. Another bloody season yet.
    (*Puts out the light.*)
  Poor old Fieldy.
OWENS. Aye.
CROSBY. Ah, well … this time tomorrer.
OWENS. Have no more bloody worries then.
    (*They laugh.* CROSBY *puts his arm round* OWENS. *They go.*

*Pause.*
HARRY *comes in, looks round. He carries a sweeping brush.*
*Starts sweeping. Picks up one or two bits of tape, etc. Turns on the Tannoy: light music.*
*Sweeps.*
*The remaining light and the sound of the Tannoy slowly fade.)*

## CURTAIN

## PENGUINEWS *AND* PENGUINS IN PRINT

Every month we issue an illustrated magazine, *Penguinews*. It's a lively guide to all the latest Penguins, Pelicans and Puffins, and always contains an article on a major Penguin author, plus other features of contemporary interest.

*Penguinews* is supplemented by *Penguins in Print*, a complete list of all the available Penguin titles – there are now over four thousand!

The cost is no more than the postage; so why not write for a free copy of this month's *Penguinews*? And if you'd like both publications sent for a year, just send us a cheque or a postal order for 30p (if you live in the United Kingdom) or 60p (if you live elsewhere), and we'll put you on our mailing list.

Dept EP, Penguin Books Ltd,
Harmondsworth, Middlesex

Note: *Penguinews* and *Penguins in Print*
are not available in the U.S.A. or Canada

# HOME

## *David Storey*

*Home* is David Storey's moving vignette of life in a mental home. It opened in London in July 1970, shortly after his previous play, *The Contractor*.

'Improbable as it might seem that any author could in the space of a few months write two plays equally haunting and moving, equally concerned with a deep and inexplicable, or at least unexplained, sadness, this is what Mr Storey has achieved' – Harold Hobson in the *Sunday Times*

'As a view of crippled lives and wintry tenderness between them, the play is beautifully spare and sustained in tone' – Ronald Bryden in the *Observer*

'Beautiful . . . David Storey's plays become ever more refined, as austere as Pinter or even Beckett, but nearer to common experience, almost naturalistic' – D.A.N. Jones in the *Listener*

*Not for sale in the U.S.A.*

# IN CELEBRATION/THE CONTRACTOR

*David Storey*

David Storey, novelist turned playwright, achieved out-standing success in 1969 when both *In Celebration* and *The Contractor* were staged at the Royal Court Theatre under the direction of Lindsay Anderson.

*In Celebration* explores family and class conflicts in a Yorkshire mining town when three brothers return to celebrate their parents' fortieth wedding anniversary.

'A rich and deeply satisfying work . . . Mr Storey's greatest strength is his eye for social detail' – *The Times*

In *The Contractor* a self-made business man supervises the erection of a marquee for his daughter's wedding.

'A subtle and poetic parable about the nature and joy of skilled work, the meaning of community and the effect of its loss' – Ronald Bryden in the *Observer*

*Not for sale in the U.S.A.*